Yeah... Me Too

What He Said That Changed EVERYTHING

By: Sara P. Cozi

TABLE OF CONTENT

DEDICATION

For James, who always saw the beauty in me even when I couldn't see it myself. Thank you for loving me enough to help me find the real me.

For Diane, who has walked this path with me and held my hand when times were tough. Thank you for always accepting me for who I am, loving me, and supporting me on my journey.

The two of you mean everything to me. I am blessed to have you in my world.

INTRODUCTION

Why I Wrote This Book

This is the story of an amazing woman. As a teenager, she was beautiful. She had long, wavy brown hair and beautiful eyes. Her complexion was unblemished and smooth, with lips that always appeared as if she were wearing lipstick, even though she never did. Her cheeks had a natural blush that other women admired and men loved. Her shapely, long legs were always tanned and lean, and she had an enviable hourglass figure. Her body was truly amazing.

The beauty wasn't only on the outside. She was kind and loving, with a huge heart. She was always smiling, laughing, and making those around her feel full of life. Longing to please everyone, she was quick to do whatever others asked of her. Her quick wit, stable logic, and fantastic sense of humor meant everyone loved being around her.

As you can imagine, she caught the attention of the boys and men around her. She was one of those girls that the other girls wanted to spend time with and boys wanted to date.

Having possession of a very intelligent mind and a love of learning new things, she did well in school. Always at the top of her class, she was one of the favorites of every teacher. She was not just smart; she was also determined and took her responsibilities seriously. She was an excellent planner and nothing she wanted to do or have escaped her. That laser focus created predictably excellent grades. The academic excellence combined with the ability to work two jobs while she went to school, balancing all three perfectly, showed her talent to create the big picture in her life. The competence she displayed in everything she did was incredible. As I said, she was amazing.

There was one major problem, however: she didn't recognize any of this in herself. She never saw herself as the beautiful, amazing, powerful young woman that everyone loved. In her mirror, what was reflected to her was a broken, fat, ugly girl who was intelligent but unloved and unlovable.

The reflection she saw was the result of many forms of abuse. The abuse began earlier than she could even remember and touched every part of who she was. Her life as a victim of other people's pain and dysfunction created a picture of someone that she never was, but she could see nothing else.

I was that young woman. My life was filled with pain and self-hatred. I saw no beauty, no value, no love. I saw nothing but darkness. I knew my heart was good, but it didn't translate to the reflection I saw in the mirror.

As I type these words, tears stream down my face for that sweet, broken young woman. I thought I had healed those wounds, but I realized that my heart was still broken about who I was back then. There was so much pain and misery that it really is kind of astounding that I survived at all.

In this book, I will share with you who I was, how I became that person, and the miracle that allowed me to break free from my past. It shares the miracle that brought me to the woman who sits here typing these words. The woman who looks in the mirror today sees the beauty within herself. No gift is more beautiful in this world than the one I received.

The years have brought some wrinkles to my face, some extra weight, and even legs full of varicose veins. But I am still beautiful. I am powerful. I am funny and smart and witty and loving. I give more than I take. I am generous and kind with both my time and money. I am a true friend who is fiercely loyal and always stands up for what is right, even when it costs me. I am hard-working, dependable, and focused. I have amazing gifts, including the ability to see the very best in other people. I inspire others to become a better version of themselves. In short, for the first time, I love myself. I see myself for who I truly am. It is amazing to live every day with someone that I love and fully accept when I look in the mirror.

I invite you to join me on this journey. I can't promise you that it will be easy to read. For most people, it will hit some deep emotional areas. I don't delude myself to think that I am the only one who suffered the abuses I did. I am positive that at least one person reading this suffered much worse abuse. I won't tell you these stories to evoke pity or to be dramatic. They are simply the things that created who I was, helped me learn about myself, and supported me in reaching the person that I am.

The good news is that the ending is a happy one. So come join me as I walk through the years to move from being a victim to being a victor. I hope that in these pages, you find the path to your own personal victory.

CHAPTER 1
Early Memories

I guess the best place to start is always the beginning. I was born in Banbury, England, the youngest of eight children to a stay-at-home mother and a father who was in the Air Force. As you can imagine, with eight mouths to feed on an Air Force sergeant's pay, we were poor. We never went hungry, but there were never any extras.

We moved back to the US when I was two and a half years of age, so I have only two memories of life in England. Both, however, tell a lot about who I was even then. The first memory is of my older brother, Michael, pulling me in a wagon. I had four older brothers, but Michael was always the big brother I went to for protection and support. He was the place where I sought safety in my very scary world. Throughout my younger life, he was always my hero.

The second memory is of boarding a plane to come to the United States. Back then, there were no jet bridges. I remember walking with my family across the tarmac to the bottom of this huge set of stairs going up into the plane. The steps came up to my waist, and there was a long line of people behind us, so my father tried to pick me up. Immediately, I pushed his hands away and yelled at the top of my lungs, "I'LL DO IT MYSELF!!!" That was and is still me. I have always been fiercely independent and always faced a challenge head-on. It has served me well in my life but has caused me some challenges as well. At the same time, it was a reflection of my feelings toward my father. You will understand more of that as you read.

When we moved to the States, a lot of things happened that I don't remember. I learned them through family stories and recovered hidden memories as I got older. Like all memories, they can be disjointed at times, but each holds the keys to who we become. I will attempt to make my memories as easy to understand and as logical as I can, but bear with me. Remember, I was just a little girl.

One of the memories that I have as a very young girl was the first time I went for a ride with my dad when my mom wasn't there. I know that sounds like an odd thing to remember, but it was HUGE for me. See, I was terrified of my father. I don't remember it, but my mother said I used to scream like someone was murdering me if they left me alone in a room with him. Why? Well, to put it bluntly, my father used to beat the shit out of my siblings and mother, among other things.

Let me share a few examples with you so that you can understand better why I would have that reaction to my dad. He once tried to run my brother over with a car. Another time, he beat my brother, and when my brother refused to cry, my dad hit him in the head with a hammer. He used to line up all the kids once a week and whip us all with his belt. If you dared to say you hadn't done anything, he responded that he was sure there was something you had done that he hadn't caught, so the punishment was for that.

As I said, I don't remember all of those events because I was so young, but I did witness them, so they affected the way I viewed him. No wonder I was so terrified of him. So, the day that I rode in the back of the pickup truck with my siblings without my mom around was a huge deal for me. I was facing the monster alone. It was my first real step toward "being a big girl."

Another memory that comes back to mind often is sitting

at the kitchen table on my brother-in-law's lap. He was married to my sister Joyce, who was twelve years older than me and was my second mother. She actually spent more time with me than my mother did.

To get away from my father, she ran away at 16 and got married. On the day of my memory, my sister and her husband had come to visit. Joyce was at one end of the table, and my dad at the other. Joyce's husband, Sammy, and my mom were sitting beside each other at the side of the table. I was in Sammy's lap. He had his finger inside of me, masturbating me. I can't imagine how often he had done that before because it all seemed perfectly normal to me. To think of it now makes me physically ill, but back then, it was obviously a normal part of my daily life.

To be violated like that while I was sitting with three people who should have protected me created the perception in that little girl that nothing and no one was safe. This belief followed me for most of my life. As a result of this experience, I accepted this behavior as what I should expect from those who "love" me, and it is what defined my perception of my value for most of my life.

Is it any wonder I never felt safe in my world? There was violence everywhere, and no one was protecting me, or so it seemed in my young mind. Anything could happen to you. You could be beaten, sexually abused, or even killed. That was a real fear as well. I learned it was a possibility when my father and oldest brother were arguing one day. My father pulled out a gun and held it to my brother. My mom jumped between them, and I stood in terror, thinking that I was going to see both my brother and mother murdered in front of me. He was a bully and would likely never have actually done it, but I didn't know that at the time. It wasn't the last time that particular scene was played out in my family, either. It occurred a second time with my brother Michael. Each time one of these things happened, my world felt a little less safe.

Another vivid memory is me lying in bed at night. My bedroom was right next to the living room, and I could hear Johnny Carson on the TV. That memory is so clear, and I often wondered why I would remember something so seemingly unimportant in such a vivid way. I spent my entire adult life until very recently using it as an example of how I have always had a hard time falling asleep at night. I had been able to sleep soundly as long as it was light outside, but as soon as it got dark, I was wide awake. So, there I was as a little girl lying there listening to Johnny Carson at 11:30 at night. Another night of it being difficult to fall asleep. Apparently, I was half-vampire. If only it had been that simple.

The truth of my sleeping difficulties wasn't revealed to me until I was 56 after seeing a Post-Traumatic Stress Disorder (PTSD) specialist therapist for almost 20 years. We had talked about so many things, so much trauma, so much abuse. I really didn't think there was anything left to uncover. During one session, however, I finally allowed myself to see behind the wall of that memory. It wasn't that I was lying there awake just because I couldn't sleep. My father was sexually abusing me, and my mom walked in and saw him. She said nothing. She just walked out and closed the door behind her.

This had remained hidden for so long because I absolutely adored my mother. She had been my best friend for my entire adult life. We did everything together. We lived in the same house, and I took care of her until the day she died. It's why I couldn't recall it before then. I couldn't allow myself to see it until after she died. Acknowledging and facing a betrayal on that level was just more than I could bear while she was still alive.

It also made sense of so many things that I hadn't understood before. It wasn't just the violence of my father that terrified me. It explained why he insisted that I kiss him goodnight every night before I went to bed and why doing it made my skin crawl. I HATED it.

It even explained the one vivid nightmare I had as a child that I never forgot. I had run into my bedroom, trying to get away from a monster that was chasing me. I wanted to climb out the window, but when I opened the door, there was a maze in the room, so I couldn't get away from that monster that I now realize was my father. It was the room where he captured me in both the dream and real life.

The sexual abuse was simply one more reason why life was so scary, and I felt so unsafe. Even before I remembered him sexually abusing me, I was doing an exercise in a book that had me draw an overhead view of the house I was raised in and pull up memories from each of the rooms in my house. I had a revelation that day. This was supposed to be the place where I was safe. It was the most dangerous place I have ever been in my entire life. It was a house of horrors for me. It was the place that left me vulnerable and broken for most of my life.

Learning the dark secrets in the closet is never easy. It is unsettling to learn things that you never even suspected, to say the least. There are reasons why these things happen. My mother, for example, was as much of a victim as we were, and as an adult, I understand that. As a child, however, nothing makes sense. I was simply a scared, abused little girl who didn't know where to turn.

Those things that happen to us, particularly before we are eight years old, play a huge part in the adults that we become. I was no exception. What I understood of the world as a child is that it is not safe, and even those you love the most can't or won't save you from the evil that seems to lurk around every corner. Is it any wonder that I would end up as the girl I described in the introduction?

Please go to <u>www.yeahmetoobook.com</u> to watch a short video with some behind-the-scenes information not included in the chapter.

What I Learned

Regardless of whether we perceive a situation as good or bad, there are always lessons that we learn from our experiences. At the end of each chapter, I will share with you a condensation of what I learned from the events in the chapter in the hopes that something I learned will support you in your own journey.

I learned to be independent and strong. By living in a world where I could trust almost no one, I learned to take care of myself. I came to understand that I was capable of dealing with the world around me by being strong and resilient. Standing on my own two feet and taking care of myself served me well for the first part of my life when I felt like no one else could be trusted until I was able to grow and evolve into someone who could trust the world where I lived.

CHAPTER 2
Is This Love?

If you've never been exposed to someone who has experienced sexual abuse, let me share some insights with you. The physical act isn't the part that normally does the damage. It is the mental and emotional scars that create lifelong damage. There are multiple reasons for that, and volumes have been written on it. I can't speak to everything. I can only share what it created in my life.

As I stated earlier, the first thing it did was to send the message to me that sex is how someone who supposedly loves you expresses that love. If you want love, you should expect to be touched and used sexually. It creates a strange relationship within you to attempt to understand your value in the world. I felt, as most abuse victims do, that if I had sex with someone, they would love me. As if sexual acts create love. Logically, that makes no sense, but to someone who has had this experience, it is the only thing that does make sense.

As a result of the wrong belief system, I began seeking sexual interaction with boys and men because I was seeking love. The equation in my head was that if we had sex, they loved me. If we didn't have sex, they didn't love me. That, combined with the other abuses that left me feeling unloved, meant I sought out that attention and "love." At the time, it made life and love very black and white.

If you haven't lived it yourself, I know that is difficult to understand, but the simple act of touch becomes confusing. For me, the sexual abuse was from men, so any time a man touched me in any way, I had a very heightened reaction. It put me on high alert. Is this someone who wants to "love" me? As a result, I presented myself sexually to any man outside my family who did something as simple as putting a hand on my shoulder. That is a trait very common among abuse victims. It is also what allows sexual predators to quickly and easily identify you as an easy target.

A second result, at least for me, was guilt and shame. I was far too young to even realize that what was being done to me was wrong. As I said, the one memory I have carried throughout my life of being abused was with Sammy. At the time, it seemed perfectly normal, so it had obviously been taking place for quite some time. I am equally sure that he, like all abusers, told me to keep it a secret and that I would get in trouble if anyone knew. So, the message that was received was that I was the one doing something wrong, not him, which began a whole cascade of feelings of guilt and shame so common in victims of sexual abuse.

To compound the problem, the human body is designed for sexual interaction to feel good. That added another layer of guilt and shame. I was doing something wrong, and my body was responding to the stimulation. It left me feeling like I was a bad girl who deserved whatever happened to me.

As I got older and entered into my adult life, I understood that he was the one who had done something wrong, but my guilt remained. I believed I must have done something to make him do those things to me and that I must have wanted him to do them because it felt good. Both were totally untrue, but that is how sexual abuse makes the victim feel, no matter how illogical the thought is.

I have talked to many others who have been abused, and their stories are the same. The message you carry is always, "It must have been my fault." As a result, you carry that pain, guilt, and shame with you to every part of your life, and it darkens everything you touch.

It showed up strongly in every area of life, but especially in the area of love and sex. What happened to me happens to most abuse victims. The line between love and sex is very blurred. I felt that it wasn't possible to have one without the other. The other part that was very odd, as I said, was that, in my mind, sex created love. If you have sex with someone, you will fall in love with them, and they will fall in love with you. Convoluted, I know, but in the mind of a child, it made sense and stayed buried deep in my subconscious far into adulthood. It's not a thought pattern you change due to cognitive development. It is not something logical that will go away regardless of how smart you get. It is a deep emotional wound that must be healed, and until it is healed, it colors everything and affects all of your actions.

As a result, I started having sex very young and was very promiscuous. That only added to the guilt and the shame. Only bad girls had sex early and continued having it with multiple partners through their teenage years and adulthood. The guilt and shame are like a sickness that keeps feeding itself over and over. One violation created a pattern of self-deprecating behaviors that just kept spiraling. Before long, it becomes an almost impossible shame to overcome.

I had deluded myself as I was writing the beginning of this that I could just talk about this subject and not delve into it deeply. You see, even after all the work and self-growth, a small sliver of shame is still inside me. It's time to cut the head off the dragon, face the demons, and bring everything out into the light of day so that those of you reading this can understand the depths of my pain and sadness and how I have been transformed. My wish is that this honesty and vulnerability will help others slay their own demons.

First, let me answer the question that you are probably thinking about. The answer is no; I never told anyone about the sexual abuse. Like a good little victim, I kept it quiet. I didn't want anyone to think that I was a bad girl. So, it was a wound that festered inside me until I was in my 20s.

Then, one day, I was at a friend's house. Her mother was trying to convince another friend of ours to read a book called "The Courage to Heal," about recovering from childhood sexual abuse. Our friend kept insisting she didn't need it, and I quietly spoke up and asked if I could borrow the book. Everyone in the room turned to me in shock. It was the first time I ever cracked the door open and let a sliver of light in on that dark secret.

I read that book cover to cover in a single day. For the first time, I understood some of my behaviors. I wasn't alone. I wasn't crazy. I wasn't a horrible person. Other people not only experienced what I did, but they also responded in many of the same ways. For the very first moment in my life, I realized that I was a victim, not the perpetrator of a horrible act. But still, I kept it hidden from everyone else because even though I understood it wasn't my fault, it didn't erase the shame.

It took the birth of a child to get me to open the door wide and expose the truth. It wasn't my child that was born. It was the birth of my pedophile's first grandchild.

He and my sister had a son. When their son was grown, his wife gave birth to a beautiful little girl. When I found out it was a girl, cold chills went through my body. All I could think about was what Sammy had done to me, and as much as I didn't want to tell my sister, my mom, or my nephew, I would rather have died than allow him to touch that precious baby. I had the power to save her from living the pain that was my life, and regardless of the cost, I knew I had to do it.

I gathered every bit of courage I had and told my mom and my sister. I couldn't tell my nephew about his father. I chickened out, but I made my sister promise to tell him never to let Sammy touch her. I told them about the memory at the kitchen table and that even them being in the same room wouldn't stop his monstrous behavior.

You may be wondering how they reacted when I told them. I'd love to tell you that there were tears and tons of support, but remember that they lived in the same dysfunction I did. We discussed the one time I remembered him molesting me. I discovered later that both of them had also been molested. They had never dealt with their own abuse, so they had no idea how to deal with mine. They both said they were sorry it happened to me, and that was pretty much it. It was after sharing my truth with them that I started getting therapy. The wounds could finally be cleaned out to begin the healing process.

I've gotten ahead of myself, though. I promised to share with you the ugly details of how this abuse affected me in terms of love and sex. Again, I remind you that sharing this isn't about evoking pity or creating drama. It is about understanding who I was and how that person was created; only by understanding can you understand how powerful the transformation that occurred in my life was and continues to be.

When I was nine years old, I used to have a fort in the woods with several friends. If it rained, we all took turns checking on it to make sure it wasn't leaking. On one rainy day, I went out to check on it, and so did one of my friend's older brothers, who was fourteen.

We were both inside the fort, making sure there were no leaks, and he suggested we play a game of truth or dare. I didn't know what it was, but I went along with it. One thing led to another, and I ended up losing my virginity that day. The irony of it was I didn't even know what we were doing. He dared me to let him, and I said yes. There was no emotion. Of course, with my past, why would that have even been a consideration?

I was so oblivious to what had happened that I remember having our sex education class three years later. When the instructor described intercourse, I remember thinking, "I've done that." It breaks my heart to think about it now. One more male that took advantage of me.

I was twelve when it happened next with a grown man who was dating my friend's mother. That was followed by many more, and the story was almost always the same. Men who were substantially older than me, many of them married, took advantage of my innocence, confusion, and desire to feel loved. When you have been sexually abused, it's like any man who is sexually deviant can see it in you from a mile away and immediately focus on you. I always agreed because I was seeking attention, acceptance, and love. In my mind, if you recall, if I had sex with them, then they would love me. All I ever wanted was love.

When I was 16, something very different happened, but I didn't even know it at the time. I didn't realize it until 40 years later. One of my brother's best friends, James, came home on leave from the Air Force. He and my brother were eight years older than me, so when he returned from active duty, my brother had already moved out of the house. I told James that Mike didn't live there anymore, but I would tell him how to get to Mike's house. James said that he wasn't there to see my brother; he had come to see me.

James was at my house all the time growing up. He used to work at my parent's store. He was like a part of my family, so I didn't find it odd at all that he had come to see me. He was home visiting old friends.

We went into the house and started playing darts as we always did. I remember it now as if it were yesterday, even though it's been 40 years. He was holding the last dart in his hand and turned and looked at me sitting on the dryer. He said, "I've been waiting for you to be old enough to tell you this. I love you. Will you marry me?"

You could have knocked me over with a feather. No, in all honesty, a feather would have been overkill. A speck of dust would have been sufficient to knock me off that dryer. I had no clue whatsoever that he had any interest in me at all. I always assumed that he had thought of me as just Mike's kid sister. He had always been a perfect gentleman and never, ever touched me inappropriately. Since physical touch and sex were the way I understood love, it never even entered my mind that he was interested in me.

I was shocked, to say the least. Thoughts raced around my head at a million miles an hour. And, of course, I came to the only conclusion that made any sense at all to me in my broken heart and warped reality. He just wanted to get laid.

I stammered out that I was only 16 and wasn't thinking about marrying anyone. Even though I wanted love, to me, the idea of marriage was absolutely abhorrent. I wanted nothing to do with being married to someone so they could beat me like I had seen happen to my mom and my sister. I told him I was going to college and be a doctor so I couldn't marry anyone and that my father wouldn't let me, and anything else I could say to keep him from thinking about asking me again.

I'm sure the question in your mind is, did I have sex with him? The answer is no. I am positive I would have if he had tried but James was a perfect gentleman. We went into the living room where. James and I lay on the floor with my back to him. He wrapped his arm around me and just held me as we watched TV. It was the only time in my life, up until recently,

19

that I ever had anyone just hold me and make me feel safe.

In reflection, I realized later that he never even attempted to touch me sexually. He just held me. When he left, he kissed my cheek and said goodbye. I never heard from him again. To my mind, at that time, that was confirmation that he just wanted sex, and when he didn't get it, he was finished with me.

There were other men in my life who cared about me, too. I just didn't recognize it. My self-esteem was so low that I couldn't imagine any man wanting me. All I could see when I looked in the mirror was a fat (I was always a little on the heavy side), ugly girl. The combination of sexual abuse, which twisted my perceptions, and the constant messages from my father that I was useless, worthless, and lazy left deep scars. Add to that the typical kid teasing of my brother, calling me fat, and you can see why it left me thinking there was nothing in me worth having or wanting.

I look back now and realize just what a warped sense of reality I had. I see pictures of myself. I was beautiful. I was smart. I was funny and witty. I had a wicked sense of humor, tons of fun, and a huge, kind heart that only wanted the best for everyone around me. When you are abused, however, the lies and pain overshadow everything positive.

I think back on relationships that weren't what they could have been. I remember John, who worked at the pizza shop with me. He used to sing to me all the time. Every night, he would come back into the kitchen and talk to me until our boss yelled at him to get back to work. He always wanted me to go everywhere with him. He bought me presents. He used to come up behind me and kiss my neck all the time. He tried to tell me in a million ways that he was interested, but I could see none of them. My walls were already so high to keep me safe that he nor any other boy or man dared come out and tell me they were interested. He was this incredibly handsome guy that all the girls wanted. How could he possibly want me? I just thought he was being a friend. It is so sad that I was so young and yet already so completely broken.

You may be wondering if that young girl ever had any real relationships. The answer is both yes and no. I had relationships with boys/men, but they were not healthy or normal in any traditional sense. It was always me trying to create something that wasn't really there.

My first "boyfriend" was when I was twelve years old. He was fourteen and lived in my neighborhood. We talked on the phone every day, but he was constantly telling me about his last girlfriend and how he still liked her. I was always trying to live up to her. I tried to get him to have sex with me (remember, my mind said that would make him love me.) He wouldn't, as he told me years later. He was young and scared. After a year, he asked another girl out on a dare. I found out and broke up with him. That was as normal of a relationship as I ever had. Sad, huh?

After that, it was me creating relationships in my head that were not based in reality. They were men that I had sex with and had feelings for over a long time, but I realize now that they never viewed me as a girlfriend. I was just a convenient and willing girl they could call when they wanted sex. They were perfect for me because there was never any real chance of a relationship, so I didn't have to confront my fear of intimacy. There were no dates. There was no hand-holding, kissing, going for walks, talking on the phone…. none of that. It was just a hollow string of sexual encounters.

After fifteen more years without a real relationship, I finally just gave up altogether. The last man broke my heart, and I completely lost hope in the idea that I would ever have anyone in my life who loved me and treated me well. I decided that I was done with love and would just have sex with who I wanted and not care.

And that is exactly what I did. I went online and found sexual partners for one-night stands. I didn't know them and didn't want to. I just wanted to feel desirable to a man for a few hours. And it worked for the moment; I felt desirable for a minute. But afterward came the guilt and the emptiness of knowing that I was nothing but a series of warm body parts to those men.

I am not proud of any of that. When I look back, I am horrified at what I did. I spent about twenty-five years going from one sexual encounter to another. Some I met a few times, but frequently, it was a one-time thing. I felt so empty and worthless.

I convinced myself that if I didn't expect a relationship, it wouldn't hurt me. I was so very wrong. It hurt me every time. I would go home feeling more useless and trashier than the last time. This horrible, vicious cycle of sexual abuse and guilt persisted. The worst part was that I was not just the victim of this abuse; I was also the perpetrator. I was abusing myself, trying to find the love that had always been missing.

I think that abusing myself was, in many ways, worse than being abused by someone else. The anger I felt was turned inward. Now, not only was I feeling emotional pain, but I was also angry at myself. That added to all the guilt and shame and created a very dark world that I lived in, and yet I went out every day and put on a happy face. My childhood taught me that it's safer to be happy, so I played the game well.

The people around me had no idea that behind the laughing, happy mask was loneliness, sadness, guilt, shame and self-loathing. When it came to faking happiness, I was a master of the game.

Please go to www.yeahmetoobook.com to watch a short video with some behind-the-scenes information not included in the chapter.

What I Learned

When you keep doing something over and over and getting results you don't like, start digging. This has been life-altering for me. Any time I find myself repeating patterns that don't serve me, I start digging deep to figure out what the trigger is. Every time I find that there is something buried there that is an incorrect message that I learned as a child or young adult. The pattern and poor results that come from it culminate in me trying to validate that incorrect message. The only way to disconnect the pattern is to examine the reason the pattern was created and diffuse the lie in my subconscious. Understanding that is empowering and gives us a place to go when we start seeing the patterns. What negative patterns are there in your life that you want to end, as well as create power and positive outcomes?

CHAPTER 3
Family Dynamics

When we moved to North Carolina, we had a store. The store was in the front, and our house was in the back of the building. That way, mom could raise us and still run the business while my father was at work. I used to think my mom was some kind of wonder woman who could raise eight kids, keep up a house, and run a business all at the same time. As I got older, I realized that she wasn't really doing it all. My sister Joyce did most of the day-to-day work for both my next oldest sibling and me. She was filling the mom role in my life while she was at home.

One of the things I realized as I got older was that there were very few pictures of me when I was young. I am sure that by the time the eighth child comes along, pictures probably doesn't feel as important. As an adult, however, it just made me feel like I wasn't as important. It was as if I didn't matter, and no one cared about remembering me. That, coupled with the fact that not a single picture was with my parents, left its own scars.

The two pictures I know about show me by myself going into the coal shed, and the other is of Joyce holding me on my tricycle. She was the constant in my life. I remember her giving me baths when I was little and teaching me to wash dishes as I stood beside her on a chair at the sink. I heard all the stories about her being the one to feed me and put me in the stroller. So again, Joyce was really the mother in my life when I was little.

As I said earlier, to escape my father's abuse, she left home at sixteen years old when I was only four. I can clearly recall being devastated and feeling abandoned when she left. I can remember her coming home to visit and giving me a quarter (a fortune back then) so that I wouldn't cry when she left. In her having left the home, I lost a feeling of security and the feeling that I mattered. To then have her husband molest me only added more pain and confusion to my life.

About the same time that she moved out, my parents decided to build a new store on the lot we owned beside our house and remodel our home to give us more room. It was much needed. Until then, Mom and Dad slept on a fold-out couch in the back of the store while eight kids slept in the two bedrooms, with four boys in one and four girls in the other. Other than that, we had a kitchen and a bathroom. It was a tight squeeze, so the extra room we would get from remodeling the store into more houses was a blessing in many ways. But for me, it was also a curse.

You see, even though my sister was the one who did all the physical things, I loved my mother dearly. She was always close by. I could literally walk out of the kitchen into the store where she was and see her any time. She was there as a small buffer against my father's rages. It wasn't much of a reprieve, as he beat her as well, but I felt safer with her close by.

When they built the store next door, that all changed. She wasn't close anymore. We weren't allowed to just go to the store because we wanted to go. I lost that sense of physical connection to her. I spent some time with her there while my siblings were in school, but when they came home, they took me to the house, and that is where I stayed. My comfort and the little feeling of safety I felt when she was nearby was gone. So, at the same time that I lost my sister because she moved out, I also lost the ability to be with my mom.

For a four-year-old, that is a lot of loss and feeling abandoned to deal with. I realize now that is when I started really building emotional walls around me. I felt lost, abandoned, unloved, uncared for, and discarded by the people I loved most in the world. I was left in a home where my father could come and terrorize any or all of us at any moment with no adult around to be a buffer. The safety net was completely gone. So, I started keeping at least my heart safe, even if I couldn't keep my body safe.

Learning to not feel anything was a slow and deliberate process, even though consciously, I wasn't aware I was doing it. It started physically. I learned not to be in my body and feel things when I was being molested. Then, I could pretend it wasn't happening to me but to someone else.

I learned to shut off the physical pain of the whippings with Dad's belt. It was hard at first to not feel the pain, but after each beating, he would say, "Stop crying before I give you something to cry about." So, after a while, I taught myself that it must not hurt, or he wouldn't say that. I shut down the sensations in my own body. I didn't feel physical sensations most of the time.

That has stayed with me throughout my life. It's a hard switch to turn back on. I have a super high pain threshold as a result. In some ways, that can be a blessing, but in most ways, it isn't.

At one point, I had a fourteen-pound cyst on my ovary that I never felt until it had twisted and turned gangrenous. Not feeling the pain could have cost me my life. The other negative is that I also don't feel pleasure the way that most people do. To this day, I struggle with feeling a physical connection to anyone. It is a slow process to regain connection to your own body.

During the same time, I was also learning to protect myself emotionally by not letting anything emotional touch me. Just a little wall at first, but over the years, it grew to massive proportions. I was in my personal emotional fortress. I would only allow myself to connect to others on a very surface level. Nothing deep.

I stayed very distant on an emotional level. It was like I lived in a tower, and very few things could really reach me. Everything emotional had to pass through the thick wall that I had so skillfully constructed to keep me safe.

Occasionally, something would find a crack and get in, but most emotions were blocked and kept far away from me. That way, I couldn't feel that hurt and disappointment again like I did when both Mom and Joyce were gone from my day-to-day life. I became a little wooden soldier just going through the motions of life, trying to stay on my father's good side.

Knowing that my father's rages were easy to provoke, I did everything possible to be a good girl. I followed all the rules. I did the housework I was supposed to do. I did well in my schoolwork. I didn't misbehave. I tried to be perfect in every way. I thought that if I could just be good enough, my dad wouldn't get mad. There wouldn't be any beatings, and there wouldn't be the screaming and yelling that accompanied those rages. And most of all, there wouldn't be the two to four-hour lectures about how lazy and stupid and worthless we all were.

Those were the worst part for me. We spent hours hearing how useless we were to my father and how he was embarrassed to have kids like us. The physical beatings ended fairly quickly. The mental beatings went on for hours, and I still carry the scars from those to this very day. I am not sure those scars will ever heal completely. There is little in life that I have seen that causes wounds deeper than one of your parents repeatedly telling you how worthless you are.

With mom working at the store every day from seven in the morning until nine at night, other than to get us ready for school and cooking dinner, we were pretty much left to raise ourselves concerning things like learning about our world and how to socialize. Not that there was much socialization. We were only allowed to talk on the phone once a day for 10 minutes and visit a friend for two hours at a time, only two days a week. Other than that, we were home, usually doing some kind of work, as my father always expected a house that was ready for a white glove inspection at a moment's notice and a yard that was perfectly manicured, free from a single piece of trash in it.

I look back at that now and realize that it is no wonder that for most of my life, I didn't know how to socialize appropriately or that nothing less than perfect was good enough. I was well-trained. Much like a dog is trained to exhibit the right behavior on command.

As you can well imagine, I yearned for my mother's attention. In those few hours, she was home, she had to appease my father and give attention to all of the children. There wasn't much time for me to get my mother's undivided attention, which I craved so much. So, I used a power that we all have; we just don't realize we do. I used the power of creation to fill that desire in me.

I have always believed in God. I am not what you would call a churchgoer. My relationship with God has always been a very personal and private one. Of course, it is; that is who my father taught me to be…. private.

One of the things we all have heard our whole lives is that God created us in his image. When I was young, I thought that meant we physically looked like God. As I have grown throughout my life in faith and understanding, however, I have realized that is not what it means.

29

God spoke the world into existence. He created everything we see and everything we are. When He created us in His image, He gave us his power of creation. Genesis teaches us that first, God said it, and then it happened. Over and over, as He created the world, He said it and then it was. This is the power with which He endowed each of us. We are co-creators of our world with God. We have the ability to bring forth what we want.

I didn't understand that as a child and what I created was completely accidental, but I have no doubt that I created it with God. See, I wanted only two things in this world as a child. First, I wanted my mother's undivided attention and love. Second, I wanted to be safe from my father. Because I wanted both so desperately, I called it forth from the universe in the form of being hit by a car when I was eight years old.

I was crossing the street to go visit my friend and stepped right out in front of a small pickup truck doing about 60 miles an hour. It was nothing short of God's divine intervention that saved my life; I know that. I came out of the encounter with a smashed right hip, a broken right femur, my left tibia and fibula broken four times, and a broken left wrist. No bleeding, no internal injuries, no brain damage, and I was only unconscious for about 30 seconds. In fact, I was awake and alert before anyone could get to me. Talk about God's protection!

Due to all my injuries, I was put in traction and was in the hospital for a month. Far from the reaches of my father's rage because he would never show it in public. (He was the classic narcissist who appeared to be perfect to the world and only showed his true colors behind closed doors.) And guess what? My mom came and spent hours and hours alone with me every single day. It wasn't until I was in my mid-50s that I realized that I actually created the exact two things I wanted most.

I believe that we are constantly creating things in our lives.

We may not realize it, and what we create may not appear to serve us, but it does. Like me being hit by a car that seemed tragic to many, it gave me EXACTLY what I wanted more than anything else.

I have shared a lot of negative things that happened to me as a child, and there have been some high prices that I have paid as a result. I will share some of those with you as well, but I also want to acknowledge the fact that my childhood brought some positive results to me. There is rarely an absolute good or absolute bad in anything. It is what we choose to focus on that changes the outcomes of the lessons.

One of the positives from my upbringing is my resilience. It definitely came into play when I got hit by that car. After being put in traction for a month, I was put in a body cast for two months and sent home. It was a peaceful time at our house because my mom was always around taking care of me, and my father was calm because I was so hurt.

For most people, being hit by a car and going through months of being laid up would have been horrific and traumatizing. That wasn't the case for me. I recall a therapist once asking me to share my trauma with a psychiatrist so they could prescribe some anti-depressants. I went through everything that came to mind. The psychiatrist asked me if there was anything else, and I said there wasn't. My therapist had a look of shock on her face and said, "Sara, you were hit by a car!"

It wasn't until that moment that I realized that that event had not been traumatic for me at all. It was a positive experience. I even had the hospital reports. Every day, the nurses would make notes about how happy and well-adjusted I was. My doctor told my mother that if it had been any other child, they would probably have ended up in the psychiatric ward before it was all over. But not me. I had my mom, and I was safe from my dad. Life was good. Part of that was probably just the walls I had already created, but most of it was just having those two hopes fulfilled.

After I got out of the body cast, it was time to learn to walk again. I was in the hospital for two weeks, going to physical therapy every day and getting nowhere. They would put me in a whirlpool, and even though I begged to try to stand up, they said I wasn't ready. Frustrated and annoyed, I cried and told my mom. My dad, being retired from the Air Force, went to the physical therapy department at the base to see if they would work with me if I were released from the hospital, and they agreed.

God was awesome in giving me a doctor who understood me and agreed to release me. I began physical therapy the next day. After two weeks in the hospital's physical therapy, I couldn't even stand up. After two days at the base, I could walk on crutches. I was simply determined and ready to walk. That resilience I had learned paid off.

Over the next few years, life went on as normal for us. Mom was back at the store every day. Dad was home demanding perfection and berating us when it didn't happen. Over those years, my older siblings moved out one at a time until only Bobby and I were left at home. The two of us ran the house by ourselves while my mom worked and dad raged.

Then, at fourteen, something happened that gave me my first real insight into just how odd our family was. Up until then, I assumed that everyone's family was the same. It was my normal.

If you are like me, you wonder why a woman would stay in a marriage like the one my mom was in. It seems so strange now. At the time, I thought that was what all marriages were like. After all, Joyce's husband used to leave her black and blue all the time, too. Is it any wonder that for most of my adult life, I wanted absolutely nothing to do with the idea of marriage?

Twenty-nine days before my fourteenth birthday, my mom and dad got into a huge fight. I wasn't there, but my mom sat me down afterward and explained what was happening. Apparently, the night before, they had been to a Christmas party with my mom's boss (she was also selling real estate at that point). When they got home, my father turned off the car and started screaming at my mom about how she had been flirting with her boss and what a whore she was. Just for reference, my father cheated on my mother all the time and like most who cheat, they assume their partner is cheating as well. He kept her in the car in the freezing cold for five hours, yelling at her and berating her. Then he went into the house and went to bed.

She, on the other hand, had had enough. You see, all those years, my mother had only stayed because of the children. When she met my dad, she was divorced and had four kids. He was divorced and had two children of his own. She had lived her entire life in Cambridge, England, and he was stationed there in the Air Force. She said that when they first met, he was the perfect man. He was sweet, loving, and attentive. She got pregnant with my brother, they got married, my father legally adopted her children, and they moved to Florida when my dad was transferred. She said that as soon as she got here, he changed. He became abusive to both her and her kids as well as his own. She told him she was leaving.

He told her she could go anytime she wanted, but he would keep her kids. He said he had 50 men on base who would swear she was an unfit mother and were all sleeping with her. She was brand new to this country, didn't even have permanent residence established, and didn't know the laws. She also knew that he had his first wife committed to a mental institution so that he could get his first two kids. She had no doubts that he would do whatever it took to take her kids, too. She would rather die than leave her kids, so she stayed.

After Bobby and I were born, of course, there were two more kids to hold over her head. She had done her research in the intervening years, however. She knew that in NC, when a child is fourteen, they can choose which parent they want to live with.

On the morning after that five-hour lecture in the cold, she made some calls and then woke him up and told him she was leaving. She told him I would be fourteen in twenty-nine days and could choose who I wanted to live with. She told him that he had twenty-nine days to change and start treating her like a wife instead of a child and treat the kids like children instead of slaves. She had already set up a house to live in and a plan to follow it out.

That was one of the happiest days of my entire life! I can't even begin to tell you how excited I was at the idea of being away from my father. I even remember telling my best friend at the time that I knew what I was getting for my birthday: my mom was leaving my dad. When I reflect on that, I realize just how sad that is that any child would think that never having to see her father again was the best thing ever.

Unfortunately, it didn't happen. He did change to a large extent after that. He was still abusive, but the intensity and frequency diminished greatly, and to my knowledge, he never hit my mother again. Unfortunately for me, that meant my mom stayed. I was still living with the monster, even though he was a diminished monster. Even a diminished monster causes deep pain.

So, I lived out my life in a world of dysfunction, pain, confusion, betrayal, and abuse until I moved out and went to college. I'd love to tell you that at that time, I was free to become the amazing woman I was born to be. That, however, is not how trauma works. You carry it with you everywhere. Almost worse is the fact that you often don't even realize you are carrying it because that world of pain has become your normal.

Please go to www.yeahmetoobook.com to watch a short video with some behind-the-scenes information not included in the chapter.

What I Learned

God has given us the power to co-create our world. The spoken word is one of the most powerful forces in the universe. It carries the ability to create. When God said we are created in His image, that was what He meant. We have the power to create whatever we choose. Even as small children, that power exists. It is learning to master it that can change our world. What do you want to create in your life that you can begin speaking into reality?

Events we perceive as negative serve a purpose. If you said to anyone the phrase "a little girl got hit by a car," I can almost guarantee that their immediate thought would be that it was a terrible thing. As I shared in my story, however, it created safety and happiness for me. What are the positives you can find from the negative events from your past?

There is very little absolute good or bad in life. It is our perception that makes it so. Now, I know that will hit a nerve with some of you. It did for me when I first heard it. Let me explain. In our country, the events of September 11, 2001, were absolutely horrific. Sadly, there were countries on the other side of the Atlantic Ocean that were dancing in the streets and celebrating what happened. The event itself was neutral. It is only our perceptions and experiences that make events positive or negative. Again, I refer you back to my being hit by a car. To everyone else, it was horrible. To me, it was great because of my perceptions. I have used this fact to help me keep things in perspective. When I view something as negative, I begin to dig into it and figure out why I see it as negative. What I often find is that it is based on some incorrect message I got as a child. I take out that wound, examine it, find the good, throw out the bad, and move forward with better results. It's not instantaneous, and it takes hard work, but it is worth it. How can you use your perceptions to change your reality?

CHAPTER 4
Money Matters

One of the things that my mother and father deeply impressed on us was to work hard and get the bills paid. Everyone in our family began working at an early age. Running the family store was a given. We all had to chip in there, of course. I can remember when we built the new store next door; I was four years old and had a broom sweeping up the sawdust from the floors. We filled drink boxes, sorted the bottles and put them away, cleaned, and helped stock the shelves on Wednesday when the stock truck came. That was part of daily life for us, in addition to keeping the house clean and doing the yard work.

As soon as we were old enough, we were taught to run the cash register and began working regular shifts in the store. After a few years of working for free, they would pay us a small amount. That's just how life was in the Phillips family. Working at the store was not an option……. unless.

We lived in eastern NC in farm country. There were tons of tobacco farms around who always needed help getting their tobacco out of the fields. As soon as possible, we all got a job working in the tobacco fields so we could get out of working at the store and away from our father. If you have never done this job, let me describe it a little bit.

First, it was HOT. I mean blazing hot. The temperatures seemed like they were always in the mid to upper 90s and even into the hundreds. And being in the south, it was humid, no, it was stupid humid. It was also dirty and gross. You were covered from head to toe with tobacco gum so that you were almost black within minutes of starting work. The farmers worked from sunup to sundown with an hour's lunch break. Needless to say, this was not the most fun way to earn money. So why in the world did my whole family work there when they could have worked in an air-conditioned store? Again, that was simple. My dad wasn't with us in the tobacco field. We would do almost anything to get away from him.

As I said, though, it taught us a great work ethic. Having been raised in a house where nothing short of perfection was acceptable turned us into absolutely great employees. In every place I have worked, I have been a highly valued employee because I have learned that work ethic from my parents.

They also taught us the value of money. We didn't get a car given to us. We knew from an early age that if we wanted a car when we were sixteen, we had to buy it. It's the reason we all went to work so early in life. It also taught us to save money rather than just waste it. If it wasn't essential, Dad saw it as a waste of money. He was raised during the Depression, so scarcity of money had shaped a lot of his views on money. Buying non-essentials would trigger a lengthy lecture on the value of money, how it doesn't grow on trees, and how we should be saving for our future.

Was that, in and of itself, a bad thing? Not at all. As I said, I learned a lot about responsibility and how to work hard and pay my bills. But there was a downside. It taught us to think of money as a scarce commodity and that we didn't need to spend it unless it was absolutely necessary. It created, in me at least, an inability to see God's abundance. This is a list of things we learned about money and how it manifested in my life in ways that didn't serve me.

- "Money doesn't grow on trees" taught me that there

will never be enough money for me.

- "Making money is hard" taught me that it is difficult to get money

- "We can't afford that" taught me I need to settle for less than I wanted

- "It's not your needs that get you in trouble; it's your wants." This taught me that I should never buy anything I want - and it was important to just get by with as little as possible. Spending money on myself is wasteful and unnecessary.

- "It costs too much" taught me that I should always buy the cheapest thing available.

As you can see from these few examples, my thoughts about money were not good ones. What it taught me overall was to be satisfied, comfortable, and happy with just having enough to pay the basic bills. And that's exactly the life I settled into.

I only bought clothes when I had nothing else to wear. I always bought the cheapest things I could find. On the RARE occasion that I actually went out to eat, I decided what I wanted based on the price, not what I felt like eating. My life was a series of just scraping by.

I remember how those beliefs affected me when I bought my current house. First of all, it was a great deal because it was a foreclosure. Naturally, when shopping for houses, the first thing I looked at was the price. It was that way, no matter what I did.

The house I bought has a ton of windows. My mom, my sister, and I went out to buy window treatments. When I bought this house, the government was giving $8000 at closing to the new homeowner, so I had that money in the bank. I wasn't broke.

We went to the store, and as luck would have it, all the window treatments were on sale. We picked out what we needed to put up basic curtains in the house. Nothing fancy, just enough to get by, as I had learned growing up. The final total was just over $1,000. I cried for two hours because I spent that much money at once. CRAZY!!

The most life-altering moment about money came from a homework assignment. Several years ago, I was drawn to work with a business coach. In our first session, she realized that I had a serious money scarcity issue, so she tackled that first.

She asked me to name something that I truly loved that was very inexpensive. I told her I loved flowers. She then asked me when the last time was that I bought flowers for myself. I laughed and told her never; who buys flowers for themselves? The absolute irony was that I used to buy flowers for my mom and my sisters all the time. But I had never even considered buying any for me. At that point, she gave me a homework assignment. Before our next session the following week, I was to buy myself some flowers.

I was uncomfortable with the idea of "wasting" money on buying something that was not necessary, so I put it off as long as possible. Finally, on the last day, I thought, "Where can I buy cheap flowers?" Walmart was the answer. I could buy a small bunch of flowers for $4.97. No problem.

I went to Walmart and found a small bunch of flowers that I liked. I stood in the store, staring at them, wrestling with my inner demons, trying to convince myself that I was worth it and deserved to do it for myself.

Between my super low self-esteem and my awful scarcity

mindset, I was frozen. I knew my coach would never let me off the hook, though. I stood in Walmart for an hour and a half crying, trying to convince myself that I was worth spending five dollars on. I look back on that person, and my heart breaks for her. How sad that anyone can't see they are worth five dollars.

I finally bought those flowers, and it began to free something inside of me. I began to shed the old me and start understanding that I am valuable and that it is okay to spend money on myself even if it is something I don't need. It was okay to buy something just because I wanted to.

I will share more about where I am with respect to my financial thinking in later chapters, but I will tell you that I have bought flowers many times since then. I buy them because they are beautiful, I love them and I am worth spending money on! I also go out to eat, buy myself clothes and anything else I want to buy. The question is no longer whether am I worth it or do I deserve it because the answer to that is always yes now. The only question I ask myself is, do I want it?

Not only did my upbringing affect how I spent money, it affected how I made it. More importantly, it affected how much of it I made.

Remember that part of the message for me was that you need to be satisfied with having just enough to get by. As I have learned in the intervening years, messages like that sink deep into your subconscious brain and set a financial thermostat within you. It sets a cap on how much money you will subconsciously allow yourself to make. As a result of my parents' scarcity mindset, my thermostat was set at "only enough to pay the bills."

Guess how much money I made regardless of what job I had? Yep, you guessed it. I made just enough to pay the bills. I did lots of jobs. I was a school teacher, I ran a pool company, I was a reservation supervisor at American Airlines, I ran a business consulting company, I owned several different types of retail businesses, I sold anything and everything - and I was excellent at it. It didn't matter what the job was; the pay was always just enough.

I even sold health insurance. The income potential was stupid good, and I was excellent at it. I closed at almost 70%, which was fantastic, and the commissions were outstanding. It should have been a no-brainer for me to make $250,000 a year. But see, my financial thermostat was in play. So, I only worked about five hours a week and subconsciously found ways to distract myself the rest of the time. I ended up with an income of exactly what I had been making for twenty-five years…. $40,000 a year. Just enough income to meet the basic bills.

I am willing to bet a few of you reading this just realized that you have created your own financial thermostat. There is a cap not on the amount that you can make but that you will allow yourself to make. We are masters of self-sabotage in our lives, and this is an area that affects many people.

I was caught in a trap. I had huge dreams and goals but no way to finance them. I decided that since I was great at sales, I'd start a business as a sales coach. If you are ready for a bit of irony, get this. I knew what people needed to do and how to teach them to do it. The problem was that I couldn't sell them my coaching. Guess why?

There were two major problems with me selling my coaching. First, if I sold them the package, I would be teaching them, and with my self-esteem in the toilet, I didn't feel sure that I could get them the results. That made no logical sense since I had trained dozens of people who became great at sales with my coaching. However, these were at jobs, not my own business. Second, I was charging a lot of money to coach them.

44

If I sold too many coaching packages, I would surpass my $40,000 threshold, and my subconscious mind simply couldn't let that happen.

That's who I was financially before the miracle came that changed my life. I had a ton of credit card debt a second mortgage on the house, and I owned a business that wasn't paying the bills. I was a Master Sales Professional who couldn't sell my own sales coaching because I was so convinced that I wasn't able to do what needed to be done, even though I'd done it for over twenty five years for someone else. I knew something had to change.

So, I hired different coaches to teach me marketing, how to run a business properly, set my pricing, set up a system of how to use LinkedIn effectively, how to set and reach goals. On and on and on. I literally invested well over $50,000 trying to find the magic business key that I was missing. It didn't matter what I learned; I just couldn't get past this stumbling block, and it was driving me crazy.

You are probably way ahead of me here. There was no silver bullet to find in the business world. There wasn't a magic potion or special formula that would suddenly create an abundance of money coming in through my door because my beliefs about money and work were all wrong.

The problem wasn't the business. It was the way I had been taught to view, think about, receive, and use money. It was the way I thought about myself. It wasn't a thing; it was a THINK. There had to be a massive shift with respect to both how I viewed myself and how I viewed money to create the abundance that I wanted.

I had to learn to live with a mindset of abundance instead of scarcity. Thankfully, the way I changed both my self-image and my financial thermostat came in a single package. I'd be happy to tell you the website where you can get it, but it can't be bought. It is a priceless gift.

Please go to www.yeahmetoobook.com to watch a short video with some behind-the-scenes information not included in the chapter.

What I Learned

We live in a world of God's abundance. There is more than enough love, peace, happiness, money, success, or whatever your heart desires for you to have your share. There is no limit to how much money we can earn other than the limit we put on ourselves due to the beliefs we carry inside about money. If you are struggling financially, I invite you to look inside and find out the beliefs you hold about money. They are the reason we struggle. Once you have found the thoughts that are sabotaging your financial success, you can begin to face and defeat them. God wants you to have it all. As my mentor used to tell me, "God's people can have what they say, but they are too busy saying what they have." There is a lifetime of wisdom in that statement alone. Where in your life are you living in scarcity rather than the abundance that is available to you? Where are you trying to figure out how to "get by" when you can be thriving in that area?

Life is not about doing; it's about being. If life were simply about what we are "doing," those who work the most hours would have the most wealth. That, however, is not the reality of our world. Often, those who work the least possess the most wealth. Why? They have learned the secret that we are human beings, not human doings. What matters is who we are and what we believe about ourselves and the world, not what we physically do. If you want more money, love, power, peace, or whatever else you desire, you must first understand who you have to be to become the type of person who possesses what you want. What kind of person lives the life that you dream to have? How can you begin to be that person?

CHAPTER 5
A Weighty Condition

As I have mentioned previously, the word "fat" was prevalent in my life from early on. It has, until recently, been the first word I thought of when I thought about myself. I allowed my weight to define me and my value in the world. It's a horrible yardstick to measure yourself with. But, for me, at least, it served a purpose.

When you think about it, the body creates fat as a way to insulate itself from cold and protect itself from starvation. In proper amounts, it is vital to the body. It is only in larger amounts that you start getting negative effects. My subconscious used it in large amounts for a different kind of protection.

I was born at seven pounds and thirteen ounces. For some, that may seem large, but I was the second smallest of my mom's six babies. I had chubby cheeks on both my face and my butt and chunky little legs but was otherwise lean and healthy. So, how did I end up at one point in life at almost 400 pounds? Simple. It was safe.

Remember that most of my life has been about keeping myself safe. This was one of my subconscious mind's walls. If I was fat, men wouldn't want me and other kids wouldn't pick on me because I was bigger than them. It really was a genius move by my subconscious in an attempt to protect me. As you can imagine, however, it caused as many problems as it solved. I didn't realize it until much later in life, but I started putting on weight in response to both the sexual and the physical abuse. My young mind figured out all on its own that I needed insulation.

The physical abuse it protected me from is pretty obvious. If there was more fat on my body, my nerve endings were cushioned from some of the pain. It literally insulated me from part of the pain of the beatings. The older I got, the more my subconscious mind realized it and added even more weight.

This is not something that I read, and it's not scientific or research-based. It is simply something that I have realized and recognized as I have grown through the process of my journey. Some would call it instinct or intuition. I learned another name for it that I will share with you later in the book as I discuss my healing process.

The weight also kept me safe from being picked on by the other kids at school. Not only was I heavier than most kids, but I was also very tall for my age. By the time I was in fourth grade, I was already in an adult-sized body in all aspects. I was 5'8" tall and weighed around 150 pounds. I looked like a grown woman in physical stature. I was not someone the other young kids would even consider picking on.

As I got older, I discovered that weight gain was also an act of defiance and a way to assert my will. My father controlled every aspect of our lives. He told us what we could do, when we could do it, how to do it, and when to stop.

As a parent, there are some aspects of a child's life you must control to teach them things, but he was a control freak. Everything had to be done his way, and it always had to be perfect. Somehow, my mind grasped the concept that he couldn't control my body and how I ate when I wasn't around him. It was one thing in my life I could control. I grabbed it and held onto it like a drowning man grabs a life preserver. For me, it was a sanity preserver. It gave me at least some form of control.

Being lonely, scared, and feeling unloved, I used food for comfort as well. I learned to use the food to stuff down those feelings of being inadequate. It made me feel better. A nice piece of cake or pie soothed me. It made me feel okay and normal for a few minutes. It saved me from the horrible voices in my head that kept telling me I was nothing, even if it was only for a few minutes while I was eating.

This developed into a lifelong habit of using food to numb the pain, much like an alcoholic uses drinking to numb themselves. I have always viewed food addiction as even worse than drugs or alcohol.

You see, food is not only socially acceptable but also one of the biggest social exercises in our society. Everywhere you go, someone is offering you something to eat. You don't go to a business meeting and have someone offer you a dose of heroin or a beer. That is unheard of. But almost always, someone has doughnuts or muffins at any professional meeting.

Not only is it socially acceptable to do it, it is EXPECTED. In many circles, it is considered rude to not eat something when it is offered to you.

It is also not something you can just stop doing. A drug addict or an alcoholic is advised to stop hanging around the same people and not move in circles where they will be tempted. There is no way to do that with food. You can't just stop eating and hanging out with those people who eat. It is a requirement to continue living.

Stopping eating so the cravings begin to diminish and distancing yourself from the opportunity to eat simply is not an option. So, it is no wonder to me that I spent a lifetime battling my weight.

Last but certainly not least, my mind was trying its best to protect me sexually. The thought process behind this is based on research, and it is a very common reaction to sexual abuse. Your subconscious mind notices that the heavier a woman or man is, the less people are attracted to them. So, it concludes that if you are fat, no one will want you, and you will be safe. Unfortunately, that doesn't usually work.

Because I was already sexualized in all aspects of my life, and I equated sex with love, it created this weird dichotomy. On the one hand, the idea of being an object of sexual attention was repulsive to me. That was deep in my subconscious. On the other hand, I craved love and attention and the only way my wounded mind could think to get it was through sex. So, I literally spent every day of my life in a war with myself.

As I stated earlier, people with sexual deviance in them can spot a victim of sexual abuse a mile away. It's almost like they have a radar that hones in on the brokenness inside those affected by this horrible crime. As a result, being a little on the heavy side as I got older didn't deter them at all. I was, by this point, about 190 pounds. Others saw me as a little on the heavy side. I saw myself as fat. And so did my family. It was a word I heard all the time.

As I started getting heavier when I was young, first, the youngest brother and closest to my age started it. He called me fat. Because I had chubby cheeks, he used to call me things like Jet Jaws and Blow Jaws. I remember him and my sister Marie singing, "Fatty fatty two by four, can't fit through the bathroom door." It was kids being kids, but it was never-ending.

The other siblings chimed in as well. I remember my sister

Carol telling me that if I wasn't careful when I jumped in the pool, I'd splash all the water out. Mike told me not to jump on his raft because I was fat and I'd pop it. All of them, in various ways and at various times, diminished my self-esteem. They were kids too and didn't realize the damage they were inflicting, but my young mind absorbed it all.

My mom and dad also joined in. I can't tell you the number of times my father told me to get my fat, lazy ass up and go do one thing or another. Mom was not quite so overt with it. She would say things like, "You are getting too fat to wear that shirt," or that if I kept eating, I'd end up like a girl down the street who was about 500 pounds. Hers was more subtle, but the pain was just as intense.

Even when they were trying to be supportive, they said things that cut like a knife. The time I remember most was sitting at the kitchen table eating dinner. The subject of the discussion was how fat I was and how they wanted to help me lose weight. My oldest brother said he would pay me two dollars for every pound I lost and my brother Ralph chimed in that he'd put an extra dollar in per pound. They were trying to support me in losing weight, and as an adult, I see that. As a little girl, it was humiliating and painful.

With that background, is it any wonder that when I looked in the mirror, I only saw a fat girl? Someone who was unlovable and ugly and worthless? Someone who had no willpower (I was told that all the time) and therefore didn't deserve love and support. I was on my own.

The cycle was exacerbated when I graduated from college and began to suffer the effects of Polycystic Ovary Syndrome. It causes you to rapidly add on weight as it affects your endocrine system. In a little more than two years, I went from 190 to 389 pounds. I was no longer just a little heavy. I was morbidly obese.

You would assume that, at least then, it would stop the promiscuous behavior. I mean, if I felt unattractive before, I was grotesque to myself at this point. But that wasn't what happened. Even at that weight and size, there are still men out there who are ready to have sex with a woman whose self-esteem is low enough to sleep with a virtual stranger. And so, the cycle continued.

Eventually, I had gastric bypass surgery and lost enough weight so that I weighed 240 pounds. Unfortunately, the surgery corrected the body, but it did not fix the mind that created the body. I was still suffering from all the hurts of the past. I had been in therapy for a while at that point, so I was somewhat better but not healed by far. Over the next couple of years, I ended up back at 298 pounds.

Fortunately, by this point, the therapy was really helping a great deal and slowly, the weight started coming off. I wasn't dieting. I was healing. I was beginning to understand that I am not my past and I don't have to allow my past to create my future. I understood that the things that were said to me were said out of their own pains and insecurities. I was finally learning to love and accept myself on some level. Maybe, just maybe, I was good enough to be loved.

Please go to www.yeahmetoobook.com to watch a short video with some behind-the-scenes information not included in the chapter.

What I Learned

There are no quick fixes or magic pills. I can't tell you how many different diets I tried or how many gyms I belonged to. As I said, even the "magic" surgery didn't work. The reason is simple. Until you heal the mind, the body will do what the subconscious mind says. It didn't matter how little I ate or how much I exercised; the weight stayed because my subconscious mind still held two firm beliefs. 1. I was fat. 2. I needed the extra weight to keep me safe. Until I rectified those things, nothing else I did would ever fix the problem. It's like trying to make a car run better by giving it a new paint job. You have to dig deep and find what is causing the problem and then face it head-on. Fortunately, in later chapters, I will show you how to do that. If you are battling a weight problem or even drug and alcohol abuse, have faith. You, too, can heal. What area(s) in your life have you been trying to find the quick fix for but is worth spending time and dedication and using your faith to improve?

CHAPTER 6
Another Brick in the Wall

My experience with humans, in general, left me feeling scared, unsure of myself, unloved, and like no matter what I did, I was never going to be good enough. In short, the entire world felt like an unsafe place to be. How do you trust people when you feel like everyone, and everything is scary and that you are vulnerable and unable to protect yourself? In short, you don't… or at least I didn't.

The human mind is an amazing thing. It learns things, and we often aren't even aware we have absorbed it. Even more amazing, the mind responds to that knowledge by altering our behavior without us even being aware of the change.

I felt unsafe in every area of my life. My subconscious mind learned the lesson that the world is an unsafe place not because of things but because of the people around me. So, it did what brains do best. It subconsciously responded by constructing a wall to keep an emotional and sometimes physical distance between me and other humans. Little things at first, I'm sure, but soon, it wasn't merely a little wall. It was an absolute fortress that was being fortified constantly so nothing could get in.

As I have said previously, my mind did things like beginning to disconnect me from feeling my own body. I was physically disconnected from my world. To add another layer of safety, it also cut me off from a lot of my emotions. I didn't feel emotional highs and lows. I was numb. Sure, there were things I felt on some level, but for the most part, I didn't feel anything. Instead, I learned to think my way through life.

I have always been intelligent, so who needed emotional crap? I would see something happening and figure out how I wanted to react rather than actually feel anything. This started in my childhood and carried on into my adult life.

People have always commented to me that they wish they were like me and could just handle adversity like water running off a duck's back. Those people never realized what a high price I had paid for that appearance.

They were right, it did roll right off of me. Almost nothing bothered me. I laughed off everything like it was a big joke. What others never understood is why. It was because I felt nothing. It was like there was a black hole inside of me. The bad things never bothered me, but I also didn't feel the good things. Joy and love were just as foreign to me as pain. When I was apart from people, I never missed them. It was like they didn't exist anymore until I saw them again.

There was some vague concept of love for my family, and I did care about them, but it was never what it should have been. I learned the social norms of how I should behave toward people that I cared about. There was a huge sense of wanting them to be happy and help others, but it was in a very odd and disconnected way. It's challenging to explain. The closest I can come is to say that it was like hugging someone in a full plastic body suit. The hug and contact are there, but there is a barrier that doesn't allow you to fully interact. There always seemed to be something not fully connected, and that something was what kept me safe.

If you had asked me at that time, I would have said I had one or two friends. As I look back now, I realize that I had a lot of friends. I couldn't see it then because that would have meant me feeling accepted and valued, and I absolutely couldn't feel that at the time. But I was well-liked and fairly popular. I think that may have been because I didn't let things "bother" me. In other words, I was emotionally shut down, so the typical child and teenage remarks and antics didn't really penetrate. It's no fun to pick on someone who doesn't care, so they accepted me.

There was one emotion that was the exception. One emotion that seemed immune to my fortress. Anger. I was absolutely connected to feeling anger from other people and also able to dispense it. Maybe that's because that was my dad's emotional go-to state. I don't know. I just knew I could literally feel someone else's anger in a heartbeat and was fully capable of accessing my anger. I didn't get angry often, but when I did, it was like a nuclear bomb that I could not control. I would simply explode, and my fear, anger, and frustration would come rushing out like a bolt of lightning. It didn't matter who it was that had hit that button; I was unable to control it.

That was true even if it was my father who pushed that button. As terrified of him as I was, it was not enough to hold me back when I reached the boiling point.

One Saturday morning, I was sick and had fallen back asleep after he woke me up at 6 am to get up and clean the house. He came back an hour later and began screaming and yelling and telling me what a fat, lazy bitch I was and how I was ungrateful for living in his house. He yelled to get up, clean the house, and not just lay around……and on and on and on.

As he was yelling, I got up, went in, brushed my teeth, got dressed, made the bed, cleaned the room, cleaned the bathroom, and he was still going. Again, his lectures went on for hours. It left me feeling even more horrible than I already did from the sickness I felt. I found out later I had the flu, and that, in combination with the barrage of yelling, made me hit that boiling point.

I turned around and yelled at him that I was doing what he wanted me to do, so shut up and get the fuck out of my room. As soon as the words were out, I just knew he was going to kill me. However, being a bully, my father didn't know what to do with someone who stood up to him, so he simply turned around and left. That still shocks me to this day. Yes, shocked that he left, but even more shocked that I couldn't even control my anger with someone I was literally terrified of.

So, I spent my life in the little fortress inside my heart. I could talk for days on pretty much any academic topic, but you wouldn't catch me sharing anything important. I could and did talk to others about their emotional issues. In fact, for most people in my life, I became a surrogate counselor. They would share their situation with me, and I would give them a very intelligent solution to their situation based on pure logic. It was easy for me. I didn't have all those pesky emotions getting in the way of making rational choices in a given situation. Just don't expect me to share anything emotional with you. Because I shut that shit down hard the second it started to happen.

The times that something happened that evoked emotion, my subconscious got bricks and mortar out and started putting up walls around it. I would add another room or wing of rooms to my emotional barracade to keep me safe. Now you are beginning to understand how it went from a small wall to an absolute fortress and growing all the time. I bricked up anything that got through once. This process continued even up to my mid-fifties. Can you imagine the size by then?

Now, I will tell you that there were some really good things about the fortress in my heart. It kept me safe. If you learn to shut off your feelings, it is very hard to hurt you. After all, that was why I built it in the first place. I also didn't have to waste time on things like figuring out who to trust and who not to trust. That was a no-brainer. You trust no one! Think of all the time I saved there. I also didn't have to spend time talking to people about how I felt…. because I didn't feel anything most of the time.

Like all things, however, there was a yin to this yang. There is always a price to pay. For me, that price was loneliness. Like Superman that nothing could hurt, I lived in a fortress of solitude. While it was true that I didn't get hurt like many others did, I also didn't feel the joy. The challenge with the walls I built was that they didn't let pain in, but they also didn't let love in. I spent my life feeling cold and alone.

As I began to heal and examine this wall I built, I took off each brick and looked at what was behind it. In order to heal and feel whole, I had to face the monsters I blocked outside of those walls and figure out why they were so scary to me. Only then could I allow the emotions to penetrate into me.

When I started looking at these monsters of emotions, I found something shocking. In each case, the face of the monster was a mask. It looked like someone else who had hurt me, betrayed me, etc. But when I took the mask off, I realized that they were all me. It wasn't that I couldn't trust other people; it was that I didn't trust myself.

I didn't love myself. I didn't respect myself. I was afraid that I couldn't or wouldn't set healthy boundaries. I saw my value not through God's eyes but through the eyes of those around me who were dealing with their own hurts, disappointments, anger, shame, and guilt. I had lived my life trying to keep out the "danger" from other people when the real danger resided within my own mind. If I could learn to love and trust myself, loving and trusting others would come. But how do you do that?

How do you learn to trust yourself? I mean, let's face it, the me I was asking me to trust was pretty messed up. Would you trust someone who was abused mentally, physically, emotionally, socially, spiritually, financially, and sexually to make really good choices that would keep you safe and take you to success? It was kind of a hard pill to swallow.

But I started on that journey through counseling with my therapist. I took leadership classes to get in touch with myself. I did several specialized therapies. I did Eye Movement and Desensitization Reprocessing (EMDR) sessions for PTSD. I took anti-depressants. I read hundreds of books and attended multiple seminars. Literally, everything I could think of to dig deeper and deeper into my subconscious and figure out how to love and trust myself.

All of these things gave me some level of success. It was like peeling off the layers of an onion. Every time I pulled one off, I cried a great deal and found another layer underneath. I'd think, "Ah ha, this is it," only to realize there was more underneath that.

I am happy to tell you that I am now much closer to the heart of the onion. I found self-love and self-trust. The source of it, however, was quite shocking. It was something that I never in a million years would have guessed would hold the key. For me, it started with three little words. **"Yeah…me too."**

Please go to www.yeahmetoobook.com to watch a short video with some behind-the-scenes information not included in the chapter.

What I Learned

Nothing is more fun than playing a big game in life. Playing a big game means taking risks. They are the only way you know you are alive. Playing a big game means that you feel fully alive and get to really experience the world around you. It means feeling the full range of human emotions. They all serve us. Most importantly, it means living up to your full potential. Holding yourself small means that you diminish not only your experiences but the experiences of everyone around you. God gave you a full range of emotions for a reason, so use them all. Take chances, allow yourself to risk failure, and don't leave this world without knowing all you were born to be. If you knew you couldn't fail, what would you do today? Go and do it!

CHAPTER 7
How Abuse Shaped Who I Became

As you can tell from the previous chapters, my life was not exactly what one would call fun and free. My childhood traumas created so many negative thoughts about myself. When I looked in the mirror, the word that most often came to mind was "worthless." I am sure there are some of you reading this that are thinking, "Yeah…me too".

That very poor self-image affected every part of my life in very profound ways. A few good outcomes are the resilience and independence I learned on the journey, which were really my hallmarks. Mostly, however, I endured negative effects.

Financially, the negative thoughts about myself didn't devastate me; they just prevented me from thriving. I have a resume a mile long and have excelled at everything I have ever done. I was a top-notch telemarketing manager. I worked in reservations at American Airlines and, within the first year, was promoted to a management position. I taught a group of kids from the housing projects to achieve a 96% basic skills test passing rate. (The expectation was a 72% passing rate.) I was the top-selling insurance agent in the office even though I was only working 5-7 hours a week on average. There has never been anything that I did as a job that I didn't perform far above the average. So, how can I also say my background prevented me from thriving?

My confidence would never allow me to ask for the

amount of money I should have been earning doing all those things. I settled. I didn't believe I was worth being paid at a much higher rate. As I look back, I realize that I could have made at least ten times what I was earning if I had just asked. But I was scared I wasn't worth more. In fact, even when offered to me, I couldn't allow myself to accept more.

When I was twenty eight, I had a headhunter call me. He wanted to interview me for a position as the VP of sales in a major company that made billions of dollars a year. I would answer only to the President of the company and travel around the US training their sales departments. The base income was over eight times my current salary plus bonuses, which, with my skill set, would have far exceeded my base salary. It would have been a dream job.

I turned him down cold. I told myself then that I didn't want to relocate to Chicago, where the job was based, but the truth was that I didn't think I could do the job. Even though I was always a top salesperson and a great teacher, my low self-confidence rose up to bite me.

I also started multiple businesses. As I said, I was raised in a family that owned a business, so it is really in my DNA to be an entrepreneur. I started multilevel businesses, thrift stores, antique stores, youth leadership businesses, cleaning businesses, tutoring businesses, etc. You name it, and I probably tried my hand in the arena somewhere. I understood business, marketing, sales, and customer service. All those areas that normally hold people back were things I understood and excelled at. But I had minimal success. Just enough business to get by. Never thriving. Never excelling. Just enough to live on.

Was it because I didn't understand what I was doing? Not at all. I could have run any one of those businesses extremely profitably if they had belonged to someone else and I was on a small salary. Once again, it was my self-esteem and self-confidence holding me back. As I look back on each of those ventures, I see where every time I was either unconsciously self-sabotaging, or I was holding myself back.

In the insurance business, I was my own boss, earning $40,000 a year without even trying by only working 5-7 hours a week. Do the math: if I had just worked a regular workweek, I would have been making a quarter of a million dollars a year. But my financial thermostat said I was worth $40,000 a year, so I sabotaged myself and created the reality where that was all I made by putting obstacles in the way of working.

I am laughing aloud as I remember having two weeks where I earned $8,000 each week. So, what happened? I got sick and was unable to work at all for two months. Heaven forbid I should actually exceed $40,000 that year. Guess what? I didn't!

I am willing to bet my last dollar that some of you are reading this and saying to yourself, "Yeah….me too". Maybe not at the same amount, but there is that ceiling you can't break through. Take heart; you can use the same thing I found to break through.

My self-confidence also impacted my social life. It made me feel small and insignificant. I hid from the world because I felt I didn't deserve a place in it. I was nothing. I was fine one-on-one, but if I got into a crowd, I shrunk as far into a corner as I could get and left as quickly as humanly possible. Not that this situation happened often since I avoided any place where there were a lot of people like the plague. I simply felt awkward and out of place around even a small crowd.

The best example I can remember was a multi-level marketing meeting at my friend's house. He owned a pizza shop, and I worked there while I was in high school and trained new staff. There was an employee meeting to discuss an MLM business opportunity. Not only did I know everyone there and trained all of them, but they were my best friends in the whole world. I would have been perfectly at ease with any of them one-on-one or even two-on-one. I would have been comfortable with all of them at the pizza shop because I had a role to play there. Being in a pseudo-social setting with all of them, however, horrified me. I distinctly recall sitting in a corner and watching them all talk. I am not sure I spoke all night.

Once again, it was my self-confidence killing me. I felt I had nothing to offer. I was anxious and completely overwhelmed by simply being in a social setting, even with the people I loved most and felt comfortable with at any other time. The irony was that even back then, people were drawn to me like a magnet because I was always the one who could make people laugh. How sad that I just couldn't see it and be comfortable in my own skin. It always felt like I was wearing clothing that was about four sizes too small. I couldn't relax and be free.

And even though I was fine one-on-one, I rarely connected with anyone. I had one or two friends that I would talk with and spend a little time with, but mostly, I stayed by myself. As an adult, I shut myself off from the world. I would tell myself and everyone else that I just liked being alone with my thoughts, and I liked my own company. I said it so often that I actually believed it.

The truth was too painful to face. The truth was that I didn't feel like I brought value to anyone and that they really didn't want me around. I felt like an annoyance to others and that they would just put up with me not to hurt my feelings. Who could possibly want to spend time with someone so broken and valueless? I protected myself by putting not just emotional walls up but physical walls around myself as well and spent most of my time alone.

It also had a big effect on me physically. I never felt safe physically or emotionally. On a subconscious level, I realized that men were generally less attracted to larger women than they were to thinner women, so I put on extra weight. It served to create a barrier between me and men but also perpetuated being uncomfortable with people in general. It provided a physical shield between me and anyone else who my subconscious mind assumed only wanted to hurt or use me. As I said in an earlier chapter, this was a fairly successful tactic.

There was a second physical effect that I mentioned earlier, too. The negative self-image also kept me from feeling physical pain. My mind would go somewhere else, and it was like that wasn't happening to me; it was happening to "her." I was outside my body. I have become very adept at that because I still don't feel things in the way that others do, but I am getting better.

I am sure that many of you think that is a good thing. It actually is with regard to pain, but like everything in life, the coin has two sides. It also prevents me from feeling pleasure like most people do. I don't get physical pleasure in the way others do, either. Even though I had many sexual experiences, orgasm was something I never experienced with any man until I was in my fifties, and even at that point, it was rare. Living disconnected from your own body is an odd experience and one that is an ongoing challenge for me.

Spiritually, it had a HUGE effect on me. I have always believed in a loving God who is there to guide and protect us. Except I didn't feel worthy of His love, and I didn't trust it anyway.

I have always been told that God is our heavenly father. To me, "father" wasn't a good experience. My earthly father was abusive in every way imaginable; why would I want another one?

I wanted to believe that God was different, but my experience told me otherwise. My experience, in combination with a self-image that said I was worthless, lazy, fat, ugly and unlovable, left me not trusting a relationship with another "father."

Even if I broke through and trusted Him, I didn't feel deserving of a relationship with God. I didn't feel I was worthy of being loved and protected. I felt like an outsider, even with God.

So, even though I loved God, I was distant from Him. I would go to different churches seeking that connection. Living in the South, the message I got at most services was a God who was angry and vengeful. He was a God who demanded perfection, and I certainly wasn't that. He was a God of exclusion, where certain people or groups of people were unwelcome at the church. I look back now at the irony that the very people whom God wants to come to Him are told by the church that they are unwelcome. I find that very sad. A God or people that would do that weren't anyone I wanted to have a relationship with, and quite honestly, it wasn't the God I knew in my heart. So, I would stay away.

I kept God in my heart and in my mind. I tried to live the kind of life that I knew He wanted me to live. I wanted Him to be proud of me. I wanted Him to use me to serve mankind. But He was, like all the humans around me, always kept at arm's length. I even had a wall up to protect me from God because I couldn't trust even Him. I felt like I was never safe and never accepted for who I was because the church had taught me that he was always judging me and would punish me for my sins. How could I feel secure with that when I felt I was worthless?

It affected my relationship with my family. I never felt like I measured up. I felt like I was simply a pain in the ass to everyone, and they simply had to endure me. As a result, I tried my best to be invisible. I hid away in my room.

I would say, however, that the area where it impacted me most was romantically. As I said in an earlier chapter, when I look back, I see that there were many, many men interested in dating me. My walls were so hard, so high, and so thick, however, they never felt safe asking me out. I don't blame them. I wouldn't have asked me either.

I told you earlier about my first boyfriend. By the way, he never approached me; I approached him; otherwise, I doubt that would have happened either. After that, there were four men with whom I had an ongoing connection for a while. To call them a relationship would be a misnomer. In each situation, I was the one who reached out for the connection. We never went on dates; we just talked and had sex. That was pretty much the whole relationship. I was forty before I went on my first real date, and that was a blind date set up by friends. I was simply unapproachable.

Even when I was involved with someone, however, I was always uncomfortable. I never felt good enough. I was jealous. I felt rejected most of the time because I was so desperate for constant attention to prove to myself and the world that I really did have some value. Naturally, that neediness only pushed them away, which made me feel even more worthless. It was a vicious cycle for me.

Subconsciously, I set out to prove to myself just how little value I had. When you seek evidence of pretty much anything in life, you will find it. And I found plenty of evidence that I had no value. Oddly, now I look back at the same situations and find evidence of my value in them. As I said, we find what we seek evidence to prove. The real question then becomes, what are we seeking to prove?

The long and the short of this chapter is that the abuses I suffered had profound effects on me, many of them negative. It left me sad, broken, disconnected, and in both depression and denial. I told everyone I was happy. I put on a great face. Anyone whom you asked would have told you that I was happy and well-adjusted. It was a great mask…. for a while.

I have shared what was going on inside of me. Now, let me share the outside. I bet some of you will be able to relate to this.

First of all, I was self-deprecating. I was always making jokes about my weight. I would make fun of myself so that others wouldn't do it. I wouldn't have to hear their cruel words because I knew that hearing it would hurt me deeply. If I made jokes about it, I could tell myself it was funny even though each joke cut a little deeper into my soul.

I also made jokes about everyone and everything else around me. I was always the one who was laughing and making others laugh. It was entertaining and fun and kept everything light-hearted. I knew that people loved to laugh, and if I could use my intelligence and quick wit to make them laugh, maybe they would, if I were lucky, accept me and see some small value in having me around so I wouldn't be rejected.

I would do anything and everything someone asked of me. That was yet another ploy to try to distract people from my feeling of innate worthlessness. If you did everything someone asked of you, they would like you and want to have you around. Never mind that it was a relationship based on using me where no one took my feelings and needs into account. Never mind that I had no boundaries. They would want me around, and I felt like I belonged.

I was an excellent student in high school and college. I

always strived to be the best at whatever I did. Once again, this was so that I could feel I had some value. The teachers would like me, and my parents would approve of some aspect of who I was.

Of course, my peers noticed this and saw the advantage to them. They would ask me to do assignments for them or let them copy my answers on the tests. Guess what? I did it. They looked up to me, they respected me, and they accepted me. It gave me a sense of belonging. For brief moments, I would shine and feel valued.

I worked hard. I mean really hard. If I could do three times the work that others around me did, obviously, my boss would really like me because I was getting shit done! My coworkers would love me because I was taking some of the load off of them. Again, I didn't realize and didn't care that it was a group of relationships that was based on using me. They liked me, accepted me, and wanted me around. And that was all I wanted to feel. Accepted. Enough.

My favorite ways that I learned to cope, though, have always been the ingenious way I decided to deflect my loneliness and depression when it came to men. I simply pretended not to care. I never dressed nicely or tried to look my best because, well, why would I? I am not interested in attracting men's attention. I certainly never approached any man, and if they showed interest in me, I assumed it was as a friend. They obviously weren't interested in me romantically. So, I treated them as friends, and that's how they always viewed me too. I set myself up to lose at romance.

The walls I had up were so tall, strong, and thick that they never dreamed of actually attempting to break through them. Some would drop hints from time to time, but since I was convinced that I was unlovable, I totally missed these signs. I see them now when I think back, but at the time, I was simply oblivious to any man's interest in me romantically.

So how, you may ask, did I manage to have five "relationships" with men? Well, that was easy. I simply did what so many people with my past did. I would find a man who I was mildly attracted to who was totally unavailable and THAT was the one I would pursue. It was genius!

I could simultaneously act the part of someone who wanted a relationship from time to time, keep it perfectly safe because I knew it would never go anywhere AND prove to myself that I had no value. I hit the trifecta doing this. I created a false reality that allowed me to, once again, find what I was looking for.

It sounded like this in my head: "See, even when I allow myself to be interested in someone, they don't want me. I really am unlovable." I would steer away from any men at all for a while. When I was twenty- seven, I did this for the very last time. This last man just broke my heart, and I decided I was finished with men and dating period.

What I had learned over these "relationships" was that all men, just like my dad and brother-in-law, only used and hurt me. They weren't safe and couldn't be trusted at all. Of course, I see how I set them up to be that way, but I didn't understand that then. So, I made the decision that I was not even going to entertain the idea of a romantic relationship.

For the next thirty years, I would just find sexual partners when I wanted physical touch. Every sexual encounter added another layer to the brick wall around me and my heart. I'm telling you, by the time it was completed, that wall could have been in Architectural Digest. It was tall, thick, strong and fancy.

That was the dichotomy I created in my life. On the inside, I was sad, broken, hurting, depressed, and feeling worthless.

On the outside, everyone thought I was strong, smart, powerful, and secure. I can't tell you how many people told me how they wished they were as strong as me. If they had only known.

Please go to www.yeahmetoobook.com to watch a short video with some behind-the-scenes information not included in the chapter.

What I Learned

We will find evidence of whatever we seek. Regardless of what we want to prove, we can and will find evidence to support that belief. Two people can go through the exact same experience and have two totally different understandings of what happened because of what they are seeking to prove based on their personal beliefs. I see it so often, especially in my own past. The key is to begin looking for evidence to prove something positive rather than something negative. What would your experiences be like if you looked for evidence that you are amazing?

We are the ones who set our own limits. So many times in my past, I looked around for external constraints that prevented me from being successful in different areas of life. It was the food I ate or my lack of exercise that kept the weight on. Nope, it was my mindset that said I was fat. I wasn't working hard enough or doing the wrong job, which caused me to barely get by. Nope, it was my belief that I only needed enough to barely get by. I was unattractive and had no value, which caused me to not attract men. Nope, it was my belief that I was unlovable that kept men away. What limits are you placing on yourself that are holding you back?

Everything you ever wanted or needed to fulfill your purpose is already inside you. You just have to learn to access it. My life didn't change because of anything outside myself. I am still the same human being who experienced the abuse and the effects I have discussed in this chapter. There was no magical external force that changed my life. It was and is still just me in here. I was born with all the tools I need to live a joyous, exciting life filled with love. I only needed to learn how to access the right parts of myself. What have you always wanted to do or be? You have all the tools you need inside of you to create that reality.

CHAPTER 8
The Road to My Recovery

When something is broken, what do you do? You have three choices. You can discard it and do without it altogether. You can buy a new one and replace the broken one. Or you can fix the old one. I knew that inside, I was broken. Since discarding would have meant suicide and there was no way to buy a new me, I was left with only one option. I had to figure out how to fix the brokenness inside.

I would so love to tell you that I found a magic pill, took it, and overnight I was brand new. Alas, that is not how it happened. Like everyone else who goes through this process, it took tools, work, time, and resources. It was a slow and often painful process, but honestly, it was no more painful than the day-to-day life I was already living.

In an earlier chapter, I shared the first step. It was reading the book "The Courage to Heal." It was the book that opened my eyes and allowed me to see that what was going on in my life was the result of my abuse. I wasn't alone. I wasn't the only one who felt like this or did these things. And if someone else got through it, maybe, just maybe, there was hope for me.

It would also be great to tell you that I immediately began seeking help and support. That didn't happen either. I couldn't. My experiences as a child taught me you can't ask for help, and if you did, you would be betrayed and hurt. Since I had never shared with anyone that I had been sexually abused, I certainly couldn't talk about it.

I continued to suffer in silence until my abuser's granddaughter was born. That was a huge turning point. As I stated earlier, it was something I had to share with my mom and my sister to protect my niece, regardless of any cost to me. The courage to do that started the ball of recovery rolling.

Finally, I was able to say the words out loud to people. One of my sexual partners became a friend, and I told him about what had happened to me. God works in mysterious ways. This man worked as an accountant at the mental health center in town. He encouraged me to talk to a counselor. I fought against it for a few months, and finally, he convinced me to start talking to a therapist. I started learning to take the monsters out of the closet slowly, one by one, and seeing them for what they were at last.

Very shortly thereafter, the therapist wanted to put me on an antidepressant. It was a flat "NO." I wouldn't even entertain the idea. Over and over, my friend who worked there, as well as another online friend who helped sexual abuse victims to understand their trauma, kept trying to convince me to try medication. But there was an absolute titanium wall between me and the idea of medication.

Then, one day, a strange thing happened. Marianna, the friend online, and I were talking, and I heard the voice of God very plainly say to me, "Ask her about the love." Now, I will tell you that it was the first time I had ever heard the voice of God, and I used to think that people who said that God talked to them were completely insane. I was shocked. It was plain, simple, and audible inside my head. It was also something I couldn't ignore.

I told her that God had just spoken to me and told me to ask her about the love. That began an hour-plus discussion about love, or the lack thereof, in my life. We talked about the fact that I wouldn't allow anyone to love me because it wasn't safe. My experience was that people who love you are the ones who hurt you. We talked around a big circle, and the answer God wanted me to find was finally revealed. I was afraid to take medication because it would allow me to begin to love myself. If I loved myself, it would allow God to love me, but I wasn't worthy of His love and didn't trust it. I can recall sitting in front of my computer understanding that as if it were yesterday. It was life-changing because it started me allowing some form of love into my life.

At my next appointment, I began talking about taking antidepressants. I found out that trauma causes physical changes in the brain that either don't allow you to make enough serotonin, which is the chemical that makes you happy or that if you are making enough, your receptors for this chemical don't absorb it properly. I wasn't crazy or broken! I simply had a medical situation created by years of abuse and trauma.

Since we had no way of knowing if it was the lack of producing serotonin or the inability to receive it properly, we had to try several different kinds of medications. Within a few months, we found the right one, and the lights began coming on inside of me. Things started seeming brighter and clearer. When I smiled, it was because I genuinely felt good, not just because of the mask that I had worn for so long. I started sharing a little bit of the real me with those close to me.

I saw that counselor for about a year and worked through at least the basics of my sexual trauma. I began understanding how trauma affects people. I was able to begin talking about my abuse without crying every time. I began to see it as something that had happened but wasn't still happening. My feelings of guilt slowly decreased.

Guilty? Anyone who hasn't suffered sexual abuse will find that an odd word. Those who have experienced it understand exactly what I mean. It causes you to feel that you somehow caused it. You must have done something or said something that would make a grownup do something like that to you. Your logical mind knows that you are just a tiny child, but your emotional self still takes the blame. So yes, the therapy started assuaging some of my guilt about "allowing" two grown men to take advantage of a tiny little girl. The human mind is baffling.

After a year, I moved. Now, logic dictates that if you are doing something and it is starting to help, you should continue doing it. However, we are not always logical. I told myself I was better and didn't need any more of that therapy stuff. I did continue taking the medication, but it was another ten years before I reentered any mindset of therapy.

I had another friend who I had sex with from time to time by this point. Due to how I reacted to him during our encounters, he could see how much I hurt, how broken I was, and how desperate for love and acceptance. Jim started encouraging me to go get some therapy.

After a few months, I finally gave in and started seeing a therapist in my new town. I didn't like her, so I only went a couple of times. Jim talked me into trying again with a different therapist. I got the same result. And a third time, the same thing. By that point, I was sick and tired of talking about it and was ready to just give up and resign myself to a life of sadness. Luckily, he had a heart and refused to let me give up. He told me to call social services for a referral to a PTSD specialist, which was what I was diagnosed with. I decided I would try just one more time.

I couldn't be happier that I did. The gentleman at social services directed me to a lady named Louise Mills Dumonceaux. Anyone who has ever had the joy of being counseled by this amazing woman is truly blessed. By the end of our very first session, I had hope that there was a way for me to recover and feel like a normal human being. She explained things to me in a way I had never been told. For the benefit of those reading with PTSD or having a loved one with PTSD, I want to share it with you because it helped me immensely.

When you have PTSD, it's like the trauma sits at the very edge of your brain. Everything you see, feel, and experience runs through that trauma, and it colors everything. Anything coming in or out of your brain is looked at through the filter of trauma and abuse. That is why everything that I saw appeared so different from what was actually occurring.

She used a technique called Eye Movement and Desensitization Reprocessing (EMDR) that doesn't remove the trauma; it simply locates it in a different place so that you aren't filtering your entire world through that trauma. It is an amazing technique that helped me more than I can say. If you or a loved one is suffering from PTSD, I would recommend exploring this simple, painless technique.

I have been under Louise's care for over ten years. The irony is that when I began working with her, I thought the only abuse I had suffered was sexual abuse. The rest of it I had completely ignored and felt was normal. I guess that there are many reading this book who feel the same.

All we know is how we were raised. It is normal. It is comfortable and familiar. And we assume everyone else lives exactly the same way, so we don't recognize it if it is abusive. I thought I had a completely normal childhood other than the sexual abuse.

Should the previous therapists have realized it and helped me realize it, too? Of course, but they were only focused on the elephant that I showed to them when I walked in the door.

Louise took the time to probe and talk and find out where all the other monsters were hiding - even the ones that I was unaware existed.

She began to lift the covers so I could see the beast under the bed and crack the closet door so I could see the monster hiding inside. Once I could see them, we could start dealing with them.

The oddest part for me has been that we spent almost no time talking about the sexual abuse. The damage from that was tiny compared to disasters created by the physical, mental, emotional, and spiritual abuses I suffered. Again, if you had asked me before talking to Louise if I had been abused as a child (aside from the sexual abuse), I would have said no. That's how insidious abuse is. We can be victimized and not even be aware of it because it seems so normal to us.

That was not the end of the recovery trail for me, however. It is simply what has opened my eyes to the effects of the abuse. Louise has helped me tremendously, but I've used many other tools as well.

Books were a huge instrument for me. I have read many books on creating positive, healthy self-esteem. Some of them specifically dealt with abuse, but many others just dealt with life in general. Robert Schuller's book *Move Ahead with Possibility Thinking* taught me how to view life through an "I can" lens. *The Ripple Effect* taught me that huge things begin from tiny events. *The Secret* showed me how to manifest the life I want through the power of creation. There are so many great books out there to learn about how to have a healthier inner life.

I also attended more workshops and seminars than you can shake a stick at. Investing a few hours in such a class can be a huge blessing. Finding one tiny nugget that I could carry in my heart that made life a little better or easier was worth the entire time I spent in that workshop.

There are TONS of free workshops if you look on social media. Do they all want to sell us something? Of course! But that doesn't mean I had to buy it all. I simply went and gleaned what I could to help me move a little further down the path. If there was something I wanted to dig into deeper, I did.

Some products and services I did buy. I have hired multiple business coaches who did a great deal for my emotional health. Most business challenges stem not from a lack of business knowledge but from how we react to certain things. Those business coaches supported me through some of those mental and emotional barriers.

One in particular made a huge difference. Her name is Katia Rave. She was another of God's hidden gifts. I met her two years before hiring her. We met at a networking event. There was something about her that called to me, but I didn't know why. I would call her from time to time just to say hello. Finally, the day came when I was ready to hire her as a business coach. She and I worked together for several weeks, and then one day, as we were talking, the weight of the world came down on me. I began crying and couldn't stop. I remember her saying to me, "We are stopping your coaching for the day. You don't need coaching, you need healing."

What I didn't and couldn't have known was that God introduced us two years prior for this exact moment. She began to tell me about this course she was taking that was helping her to heal some deep wounds that few people knew about but had been running her life. She talked to me about healing deep wounds, about taking control of my life and my emotions, about becoming the leader God had created me to be.

It was a course about transformational leadership. As Katia explained to me what this course was about, I signed up online.

I didn't know where I was going to end up; I just knew it was going to be better than where I was at that time. I never hesitated. I knew it was where I needed to be. The course was $5,000, and if you recall my story about the flowers, you know that I don't spend that kind of money easily, but I was literally drawn to do it. I will say that it was one of the best investments I've ever made.

Over a few months, I learned so much about myself. The first benefit I realized was that it was like putting legs under everything I had learned with Louise. It was a real-life example of how to apply the lessons I had learned. When I was finished, I understood not only how the trauma sabotaged and affected me but also how to move those obstacles out of my way. At the end of the three-month course, I had faced fears, overcome challenges and done things I never thought I could do.

I was finally able to look at myself and understand that I am a loving, powerful, passionate woman who deserves to be seen. In short, I started playing a bigger game. Life wasn't about what I could hide from the world; it was about what I could share and make a difference.

The next step in my path was to take what I learned there and share it. A year after I graduated from that life-changing course, Katia enrolled to Captain a team of volunteer coaches to support a new group of people going through the class. She called and asked if I would like to be a volunteer coach. I had received so much from this course that I was all-in about supporting others in going through it.

Serving others often gives us the ability to grow in ways far beyond the experience when we are receiving. That was the experience for me in coaching. It was like going through the course again on steroids. In giving fully to those students I worked with, I got to experience everything in a whole new way and gain a new perspective.

The second major blessing that I received from this leadership course was that coaching created valuable self-esteem for me as my students looked to me as a leader. I got to dig deeper into who I was as a human being and how to deal with other people when they were triggered. That allowed me to support them as they walked through their triggers to the other side while allowing them to find their victory.

I left that coaching experience, understanding what I had always known in my heart but couldn't see the path. I was called to inspire and support people in their growth. It's the whole reason I had gone through what I had experienced. Only by going through it myself could I understand what others needed.

There was a third key that transformational leadership brought into my life. I say third because it is simply how I am telling the story, but in all honesty, it was the most important. And it wasn't an "it"; it was a person.

As you go through the course, there are three sections. In each section, I had a buddy. They were my ride-or-die. We both shared our thoughts and feelings to support each other in facing the challenges. We walked through the fire together.

I had wonderful partners for both the first and last sections, but this person was different. She was my partner through the middle section. She and I bonded in a way that I had bonded with few others in my life. It wasn't that we were friends that just clicked. It was far deeper than that.

In all honesty, if we had not taken this course, she would not have been a person I would have likely become friends with. Neither would I have been her choice to hang out with. But God knew what we both needed. The thing that drew us together was that we were both fully 100% committed to the processes we were learning. We were both sick of the life we were currently leading and willing to do whatever it took to get out of the mess we felt our lives were.

During the four days of that section, she was the first person I spoke to in the morning and the last person I talked to before I went to sleep after a long, hard day. We shared, we cried, we laughed, sometimes we screamed out of frustration, but we stood strong together.

When that section was over, we moved on to a new partner. I embraced my new partner, but this special partner and I agreed that we wanted to continue our path in this partnership. We agreed to have a conversation every Saturday to support one another and continue what we started. She was the one that I knew loved me and trusted me enough to say the hard shit that needed to be said. And she knew the same about me.

We called each other on our bullshit and stopped it dead in its tracks. We gave each other business and personal feedback that was honest and sometimes hard to do. We loved each other fiercely as a result. Those calls that were supposed to be a four-day partnership lasted almost three years.

There is one thing that we talked about, however, that makes her the most important thing that came out of the course. She is a warrior for God. She loves Him with her whole heart and is the first person I have ever met who really understands and knows the God that I have always loved in my heart.

She doesn't preach; she teaches. She doesn't think that anyone who says "Damn" or any other cuss word is going to hell. She understands that human beings are the ones who decide those are cuss words. She doesn't fall under the guise that churches, in general, are the key to understanding God. She knows there are great churches, and then there are churches that are about the exaltation of the church, the pastor, or the directors rather than the exultation of God. In short, she recognizes that churches are run by human beings and, like all of us, they are fallible. Her understanding of God is through the Holy Spirit.

For the first time, when talking to her, I began to understand who God really is and that what He wants most of all is a relationship with each of us. He wants us to have faith that He is there for us in every way. I understand that He speaks to us. He has a plan for us. He loves us infinitely more than we can even imagine. She taught me to listen to the Holy Spirit for the guidance I need so that I can lead a Spirit-led life. Because of her, I finally don't feel judged by God or that He wants to punish me all the time. He is my best friend and I can trust him.

There was one final brick in the path that got me to where I am today. I will share that in the next chapter because it was a massive step that I never saw coming and impacted me in more ways than I can name.

Suffice it to say that although I would have loved a quick, easy path from victim to victor, that is simply not how it works. It took time. In fact, it took years. It took effort, it took resources, and, most of all, it took courage. It is not easy to face your demons, but if a life of self-love, power, and connection is important enough, it can be done.

Please go to www.yeahmetoobook.com to watch a short video with some behind-the-scenes information not included in the chapter.

What I Learned

There is no secret. There is only a series of learnings. Oh, to have a magic pill or a quick fix! Alas, I have found there is no such thing. Healing and growing are not events; they are processes. They take time, and one step builds on the next. We learn something, apply it in our lives, and it leads to the next thing we need to learn. Be patient with yourself and with your healing and growth. Just keep learning, applying, and finding the next step on the path. What healing or growth do you want that is worth taking the next step to gain?

Seeking support is not a sign of weakness but rather a sign of strength and determination. I will tell you that this one was TOUGH for me. I think that is true for many people. Remember that I trusted no one, and my entire life was based on "I'll do it myself!" like that little girl on the steps to the plane. If you ask for support, you take the risk of being disappointed. You take the risk of being betrayed. And for me, even worse, you take the chance of not feeling capable of taking care of yourself. I didn't learn to ask for support easily or quickly. It took years of tiny steps to get to the point where I realized that it doesn't mean you are weak or incapable. It means you are strong enough to know that others can and will support you. Scary? You betcha! But the irony, at least for me, was that it created something that was sadly lacking in my life. Intimacy. I don't mean that in the sexual sense. I have learned that intimacy means "Into Me, You See." Not being vulnerable and open was keeping people from seeing the real me. It was the very thing that I needed most to heal. I needed to be intimate and open and let the world see me "warts and all." This is one of the reasons why I wrote this book. I can finally be vulnerable, open, and honest and let the world see who I really am. I have never felt more free or powerful in my life! Where can you begin asking for support on your journey?

Don't assume that there is any one thing that can heal you. Be open to multiple avenues. Just like there isn't a magic pill that creates change instantaneously, there isn't just one single type of tool that does everything. Be open to exploring lots of avenues. My journey has included books, workbooks, classes, movies, therapists, medications, conversations with friends and coaches, understanding God and His role in my life and my role in His vision for the world, and so much more. I found that every time something came up, there was growth for me. I simply had to be open and realize that if I tried it and it didn't work, what did I have to lose? Don't put limits on how you learn and experience life. I invite you to be open and explore every possible opportunity to learn, grow, heal, and take life to the next level. What types of things have presented themselves to you as an opportunity to grow?

CHAPTER 9
A Trail of Breadcrumbs

You know how, in fiction, there is always that pivotal moment on which the whole story hinges? Well, it happens in real life, too. It happened to me, and it was an odd moment that changed my life forever.

My older brother Michael, who had always been my hero and whom I thought was Superman, showed that he was human in the summer of 2022. He suffered a massive stroke. We were blessed that he survived, and he has physically fully recovered, but mentally, he lost a lot of his abilities and memories. We are so grateful to still have him in our lives.

I went to visit him and his wife Tina once he got home from the hospital. Tina decided to go get us something to eat. She asked me to talk to him about childhood memories while she was gone to try to spark some of his memories. We talked about lots of different things and had many laughs. When she came back home, we were laughing about the time that he and his best buddy James (the same one who asked me to marry him years before) had gone skinny dipping and running around the pool naked, yelling at the top of their lungs while the store was open. Those two were always up to something outrageous!

Even though Mike, Tina and James had all graduated from school together, for some reason, she was surprised to hear that Michael and James were friends. I started laughing and telling her some of the other stories of things they had gotten into. They were stories that had been retold dozens of times at family gatherings, but somehow, she had never heard them.

I guess she thought that talking to James would be good for helping Michael with his memories.

While we were talking, she was apparently trying to find James on Facebook. She asked me if I knew how to find him because he had no account on Facebook. I explained that I hadn't talked to him in forty years and had no clue where he was. We moved on to other subjects, and I went home with no further discussion of James.

God is funny, though. He lays a trail of breadcrumbs for us to follow to get to the destination He wants us to find. That is the Holy Spirit guiding us. We simply need to listen to that inner voice to find and follow our path to riches.

My first breadcrumb was the Sunday following my visit. As I sat down at the computer to place an Amazon order, God said to me, "Google James." Although I was confused, I also knew that God has His reasons for telling us things.

I had no idea where James even was in the world, so I started with the only things I knew: his name and the town we grew up in. I got a hit and a phone number. I called the number and reached not James but his younger brother John. Through John's information, I was able to find a phone number for James, who was now living in New England.

When I called the number, a lady answered the phone and confirmed that he was indeed the James who we grew up with and handed him the phone. We talked for nearly an hour. I explained that Michael had had a stroke and updated him on the rest of the family. Having worked at my parents' store and being Michael's best friend, he had almost been a part of our family and wanted to know how everyone was doing. I told him about my siblings' marriages and kids. He told me he had been married for thirty years and had two daughters and asked me about myself. When I told him I had never been married, his only response was, "Really?" and I could hear the shock in his voice.

After a long talk, it was time to end the call. I said to him, "James, it was so good talking to you again. I think about you all the time."

His response was simple but earth-shattering. He said, "Yeah…. me too," in a very soft, quiet voice. Those three words shook me to the core and changed everything in my world. You see, he wasn't just agreeing with me. I heard in those three tiny words that he really loved me all those years ago. He wasn't just trying to get laid, as I had suspected. He had truly loved me and wanted to marry me, and after all those years, the love was still in his voice.

I told him I would text him Michael's phone number and asked if he wanted it sent to that number. He said no, it was a landline, and he didn't have a cell phone, but I could text it to his wife's phone, and she would give it to him. We said our goodbyes and wished each other well. But I was blown away.

If he had truly loved me that much and still felt love for me, it changed things. It meant I was loveable. Suddenly, everything I had ever thought about myself was called into question. Could I have been that wrong about myself all those years?

I hung up the phone and sent the text to the phone sharing Michael's phone number, and then realized I had texted it to the landline. I sent another text to his wife's cell phone and figured we'd talk again sometime, so I put his name on the text to the landline.

Several days later, an odd thing happened. I am not technologically savvy by a long shot. Sending texts and phone calls is about all I do with my phone, and I have no clue how to do much of anything else with it. So, when I say this is odd,

I mean it. The text that I had sent to his landline was probably twenty or more spots down on my text thread, and yet somehow, I managed, without trying, to pin that text to the top of my text feed. I didn't even know it was possible to do that, let alone how to do it. If you said you would pay me a million dollars if I could do it again without looking it up, I wouldn't know where to begin. But there it was. So, every time I looked at my text feed, James was on my mind.

Over the next six months, I began slowly taking all the old memories out of the closet. I began to see them through the lens of someone who was actually lovable. And they all looked completely different.

During these reflections, God gave me an image that played over and over in my head. It was the image of a little girl about four years old sitting on the floor beside a huge plastic toybox. As she sat there, she took toys out one at a time, examined them, and realized that they weren't what she thought they were. It was me looking over all the things in my past that I had not seen as they really were.

I saw old pictures of a young woman who was tanned, healthy, and beautiful. I thought back to old situations where, instead of being the outcast, I was a welcomed member of the group. Times when I had not gone to places or events because I felt unwanted and realized that others truly wanted me to be there. I thought back about boys and men in my past who did things to get my attention and were interested in dating me, but I had put a wall up to prevent them from asking. I recalled being at social and business events where, far from being out of place as I had felt at the time, I was the center of attention.

As I went through the old memories, I realized that everything that I thought I had experienced had been a lie I was telling myself because that veil of feeling unlovable had colored everything. The pain that others had been in was put onto me and caused me to create completely false perceptions.

Those three tiny words, "Yeah….me too," literally changed my life. Suddenly, I saw a world of love, acceptance, and possibilities, all because one man loved me years ago and still carried that love in his heart.

Something else happened during those six months as well. James stayed on my mind because of the text at the top of my feed. Not only did I not know how to do it, but I also didn't know how to undo it. I thought of him constantly. He was the first thing I thought about when I woke up in the morning and the last thing I thought about when I went to sleep at night. I remembered all the fun we had growing up. He used to come to my house and play darts all the time. We swam in the pool. He and my brother Bobby would have contests to see who could put the most grapes in their mouth at the same time. A million fun times and laughs. I had always loved being around him. I was searching for how I had missed that he loved me and saw all the evidence that he had.

A memory hit me that should have told me everything, but that veil had cloaked it. James had bought a brand-new white Corvette when I was 13. He brought it to the store to show us. Bobby and I followed him out to the car. It was gorgeous!! Bobby asked if he could sit in it, and James immediately said, "NO, you aren't sitting in my new car." And then immediately turned to me, handed me the keys, grinned, and said, "You wanna drive it around the neighborhood?" I stammered that I couldn't drive, and we moved on. At the time, I just thought he was doing that to aggravate Bobby, and that was part of it, but not all. That's how a wrong belief can color everything. Through the right lens, I realized that he was showing me that he was trying to impress me and wanted to make me happy.

Thoughts of him were constantly on my mind, and slowly, I began to realize something. I had always had some feelings for him as well but had kept them hidden behind the wall. The funny thing about that wall was that it hid things from me as well. This was one of those things.

During those six months, I ran across an old list I had made years before. I had hidden it well because, heaven forbid, someone found out this was something I had even considered. It was a description of my perfect man. He was tall, handsome, funny, dependable, honest, considerate, patient, kind, loving, and respectful, and he treated me like I was the most amazing, beautiful woman in the world and loved me deeply. Guess who that was the absolute perfect description of? That's right. All those years that I had been dreaming of the perfect man, I had been describing James without realizing it. It's funny how God puts things in place without us even knowing He is working on something years in the future.

The healing just kept flowing over me. I valued the part James had and was continuing to play in that healing. When Valentine's Day came around, I wanted to send him a small token to let him know. I didn't want it to be romantic but a symbol of how important he was in my life, my growth, and my healing - even though he was unaware of my journey. I searched through Amazon and found the perfect gift. It was a small keychain with a dartboard on it. It was my way of saying that I remembered him asking me to marry him when we were playing darts and that it was important to me. It was a small thank you. I ordered it and had it set to him without a note. I figured he'd either understand it or not. It didn't matter; I just wanted to send it.

It was coming from China, so it was going to take about a month to get to him, and I just went on with my life. But I kept thinking about him. I couldn't get him off my mind. I was fighting this battle in my mind between wanting to talk to him and telling myself to just leave it alone because he was married. Finally, I decided one day that I would call him and tell him that the keychain was coming. I also felt led to thank him for asking me to marry him and explain that I didn't turn him down because I didn't care about him. I wanted him to know that I was just in shock and young. I realized that if he had loved me, the reason he never came back was obvious. He was hurt by my refusal, and I didn't want him hurting.

I decided to put this whole thing to rest and let God do what He wanted done with it. I was learning to lean into God a little. If James could love me, then I could love myself, and if I could love myself, then maybe God could love me too. So, I started taking tiny, tenuous steps toward a closer relationship with God.

I prayed and asked God to help me with this situation. I would call James. If he answered the phone, I would tell him what I wanted to say. If he didn't answer the phone, then God's answer was that he wanted James and me to have no further contact, and I would just move on. I called, and there was no answer. I didn't leave a message; I just hung up and, for the first time in six months, went to sleep without thinking of James.

But God wasn't done with us yet. The phone number I had for James was the landline at their house. Since I didn't leave a message, I assumed that he would never know I called. God had other plans. James must have come home from work, picked up the phone, looked back at the numbers that had called, and saw my name and number.

The next morning, I went to the drugstore to pick up my medication. I left my cell phone in the car. Now, I will tell you that I do not spend my life worrying about my phone. I never look to see who has called me, and sometimes, I have had weeks go by without realizing there was a voicemail for me. It's just not a big thing in my life. Once again, however, God was leaving his breadcrumbs. As soon as I got back in the car, I picked up my phone to see if anyone had called. I was in shock when I saw James's name there. God wasn't finished with us yet.

When I got home, I called him back. I told him that I had a small gift that was coming. He asked me why I was sending a gift, and I told him that I wanted to thank him for paying me the absolute highest compliment one human being can pay another when he asked me to marry him. I went further to explain to him the partial truth of why I had said no.

I told him that when he proposed, I was in shock and had no clue that he had any interest in me romantically. That was the truth, just not the whole truth. My heart wasn't open enough yet to be that honest and vulnerable with him, but it was important to me that he didn't think I rejected him because of him. We chatted for a few more minutes and ended the call.

A few days later, I woke up with an image clearly in my mind and an understanding in my heart. What I saw was a ring. There was an infinity symbol on the bottom of that ring, and the two sides went up and around and ended in a knot on the top. It symbolized my relationship with James. The infinity symbol represents how our lives had been intertwined in the beginning. It was on the bottom because it was something that I kept inside, closest to my heart, but where it wasn't visible to everyone else. The band represented the two separate paths our lives had taken, and the knot on the top was our coming back together to tie our lives together again. It was a wedding band, and it was confusing, to say the least.

I don't believe in cheating. I believe when you commit to someone, you get to honor that commitment. I had spent a lifetime chasing unavailable men and wasn't interested in doing that again. I had no intention of having an affair with this married man. NONE.

I also knew him well enough to know that he was not that kind of person. He has always had great honor and integrity. He wouldn't want an affair either. So, I didn't know what to do with this image God had given me. In the end, I decided that I wasn't going to do anything with it at all. He would get his gift, and that would be the end of it.

Over the next couple of months, three things happened. One was that James still wouldn't leave my mind. I had this nagging voice in the back of my mind saying that he deserved the whole truth. That part of the truth I had told him wasn't enough to remove his pain. It also wasn't enough for my healing. I needed to be as vulnerable with him as he had been with me when he asked me to marry him all those years ago. It stayed on my mind constantly that I had betrayed him by not telling him the whole truth.

I found his wife's Facebook account because I wanted to see what he looked like after all these years. One of the pictures was a photograph from their oldest daughter's wedding. The name of the wedding photographer was on the bottom. It was the same name as my own. To say I was stunned was an understatement!

I also kept checking to see if the keychain had been delivered. I kept getting notices saying it had been delayed, and finally, I got a note saying that it couldn't be delivered, and they refunded my money.

This keychain felt big to me. It felt like it mattered that James should receive it. I decided that maybe living in rural New England was the problem with delivery, so I reordered it to be delivered to me, and I could get it to him myself.

How would I deliver it if the mail system in New England were a problem? Simple, I would take it to him in person. See, this whole business of betraying him by not being fully open about the marriage proposal was eating away at me. I decided to visit him in December. I would stop by to wish him Merry Christmas, Happy New Year, and Happy Birthday and give him the keychain. While I was there, I would tell him the full truth.

At the beginning of May, my best friend, Diane, was going to Florida with me for a speaking engagement I was doing. During the drive, I saw something. I have no idea what it was now, but a bolt of electricity coursed through my body with the very distinct message that I needed to go to New England to see James in June. It was also clear that I wasn't to tell him I was coming. It needed to be a surprise. I had no idea why; I just knew that God was adamant about it. I told Diane that since she had always wanted to go to New England, she and I would make it a girls' trip.

I came home, planned the route, and booked the hotel rooms for the first week of June. A little extra irony? The only hotel within miles of the town he lived in was less than a mile from his house. God's breadcrumbs were unmistakable.

In the meantime, I was waiting for the keychain to arrive so I could stop by James's house and deliver it to him while we were exploring New England. Again, I kept getting these notices saying it couldn't be delivered to me either. This went on for two weeks, and finally, I got a notice saying it couldn't be delivered to me either, so they refunded my money. I resigned myself to either finding one in a store or that I just wasn't supposed to give it to him. That was on May 19.

On May 20, God shook things up again. The undeliverable keychain for which I had just received a refund was in my mailbox. I sat looking at it, puzzled as to what in the world was going on. At least I had it and could take it to James. Then I realized that if I got mine, maybe he had already gotten the one I sent. Taking him a second one would just be weird.

I thought about it over the weekend and decided to call him and find out. When we talked, I asked him if he had received the keychain, and he said he had. Even though it was never my intention, James and I now had matching keychains. That was apparently God's plan all along.

We talked for a few minutes about life and what was going on for each of us. It was nice talking with him. I decided to just tell him the full truth of what had happened that day forty years earlier while we were on the phone and not go visit him, but God wouldn't allow me to say it. I could not get the words to come out of my mouth. God told me it was vital that I go surprise James and that I tell him my full truth face-to-face.

I was learning to listen to God's plan instead of relying on my own understanding of the world. As a result, I decided to still stop and visit him while I was in New England. After I hung up, I got a further message from the Holy Spirit that I was to move the trip up a week.

I called Diane, and we left on our trip that same Friday. We had a beautiful time exploring Philadelphia, Boston, Vermont, New Hampshire, and Maine. Thoughts of James kept invading everything I did on that trip. Songs reminded me of him, memories of childhood, and our previous conversations on the phone kept creeping back into my mind when I was least expecting it. I wasn't sure what was going on, but I couldn't stop this train of thoughts from going on in my head.

Finally, the morning came when I had planned to visit him. I knocked on the door, and when he invited me in, my heart kept skipping beats. He was home alone and was surprised to see me. He asked what I was doing there. I told him I had something I needed to tell him and that it was something that I felt was too important to tell him on the phone. We stood at the bar in his kitchen, both of us looking down, not at one another, as I shared with him my truth. I explained about all the abuse I had suffered as a child. I explained the sexual abuse and that it had colored everything in my world to the point that when he asked me to marry him, I assumed he wanted sex. When he left, and I never heard from him again, it confirmed what I had thought in my mind, and I had dismissed the whole thing.

I cried as I told him all of this, and then I explained that when we had talked the previous August, he had changed my world with three syllables. I shared with him that when I said I thought about him all the time, and he replied, "Yeah….me too," that was the first time in my life I heard the love that was in his heart for me. And it was still there.

Once that truth was out, I was finally able to look up at him. At the same time, he looked at me, and I suddenly realized exactly why I had to be there in person to tell him all of this. I realized why I hadn't been able to stop thinking of him and why my heart skipped ten beats when I saw him and walked into his house. Looking into his eyes at the moment, I realized that I had always not just had feelings for this man. I was head over heels in love with him. I saw in that moment the man I had been waiting for my entire life. And even though he was married, and I knew we couldn't do anything about it, I had to tell him how I felt.

We spent the most wonderful three hours of my life. together We talked and shared our thoughts, learning about each other's lives. Just being there, talking, looking into each other's eyes, and sharing space created a peace in me that I cannot begin to explain. I had never understood until that morning what someone meant when they said, "You complete me." That morning, I finally did.

It was like a part of me had been missing my entire life, and I had finally found it in James. I finally felt whole and complete. There was a feeling that I simply cannot explain in mere words.

It was like I could see infinity when I was with him.

At one point, he asked me what I saw beyond that day. I told him that I wanted to rebuild our friendship, to share, and to help each other through life and that all came from my mind. Then suddenly, something came out of my mouth that I had never said or even considered in my entire fifty-six years. I couldn't control it. The words just came out. What I said was, "I want to be your wife."

Naturally, that shocked him as much as it did me. But we talked about it. He and I have always been able to talk. I explained that I hadn't meant to say it and I was sorry if I freaked him out. He said it was okay, and he liked to know where he stood. Of course, we talked about the fact that he was already married, but he also said he still loved me and had never forgotten me in all those years.

After three and a half wonderful hours, we needed to part ways because it was time for him to go to work. He asked me to come back the next morning so we could talk more. He walked me to the end of the driveway, and as I walked away, I looked back at him. He was looking at me, smiling, and I was walking on air.

The next morning, I knocked on the door. He came out instead of inviting me in and simply said, "I can't do this to her." We talked for a few minutes as he explained that he felt he was cheating and his conscience just couldn't handle that. I asked him if he wanted to stop talking on the phone, and he said no; he thought that was okay, but he couldn't be with me in person.

Even though I fully understood why, I was crushed in a way that I can't put into words. It was devastating. I was so in love with this man, and he loved me - yet we couldn't be together. One of the things I loved most about him was his integrity, and it was the very thing that prevented us from being together. I left his house unsure of what the point of this was. Why had I finally found love, real love, only to not be able to embrace it fully? I was angry at God. This was a cruel trick to play on me.

I went home angry and hurt and cried for days. My heart was broken. I decided that I needed to process things through writing and began keeping a journal. I talked to Louise. I talked to Diane. I talked to God. I yelled at God. I was just so confused.

After processing things for five days, I decided I needed to talk to him to try to figure out what all of this meant for us. I called Monday morning and didn't get an answer. I left a message on his answering machine saying that I had something I wanted to talk to him about and to call me when he got a chance. I waited all day and got no return call. The next day, he was more silence. I assumed he had decided we could no longer talk and was even more heartbroken. As much as it would hurt to only be friends, it would hurt even worse to lose that friendship as well.

The next morning, he called. He told me he hadn't realized I had called. His daughter had found the message and told him that morning. Needless to say, I was thrilled to hear from him. We talked for about thirty minutes and decided that we could talk from time to time and be friends, but no more than that. Both of us wanted to preserve the integrity of his marriage and the commitment he had made.

After we talked, I talked to Louise. She told me that maybe he was brought into my life to teach me to love myself and God, and that was his whole purpose in coming back into my life. She advised me to start opening up and looking for someone that I could love and could love me back. It sounded like great advice. I went home that evening and told Diane about the counseling session. This is when God jumped in with both feet. Diane said that she had three times received a message from God to give to me, and she had been waiting for the right time to tell me. She said that God had told her to tell me to "Take MY counsel. I want you to spend time with ME." I couldn't deny the timing was perfect.

The next day, I talked with a friend who is a coach for women who have been in narcissistic relationships. I called her because God had whispered her name to me several times, and I was following His lead. We talked about everything that was going on, and at the end of the call, she said, "I feel like it is super important for you right now to lean into God. He has everything you need. Whatever help and strength you need, use His." It was further confirmation of what Diane had said.

I started praying and reading the bible daily. I started journaling more often and being open to receiving God's love and His messages. I began to trust Him more and more. I talked with my leadership friend about this growing faith, and she began coaching me about God. She said that she felt that I was just to be James' friend and support until it was time for the two of us to be together.

Remember that all of this was happening to someone who was just an infant learning to listen to and trust God. It was overwhelming. I had to lean into God with everything. I had to put this all together in my head and in my heart. I challenged myself to trust God. And in learning to trust Him, he revealed two new things to me.

First, he said to me very plainly, "Your fortune is on the stage." This both surprised and delighted me. For most of my adult life, I had felt called to speak on the stage. I had an innate ability to share both stories and inspiration. I now saw it was not just an innate ability. It was a gift from God.

Immediately, however, I began to stress out about what I would talk about. I had no clue. God instantly calmed me by speaking to my spirit that He would write the presentation material, and I would just deliver it. At that moment, I had complete peace about my career path.

When that peace came, He gave me an image. It was me on a stage. I could see myself from behind in a red dress with a diamond tennis bracelet on. As I finished speaking, I turned and walked off the stage into James's waiting arms, and he smiled proudly. It didn't feel like a daydream. It felt like prophecy. I knew that if I learned to fully trust and believe in God and how to have real faith, then God would create health, wealth, and love in my life. How could I resist?

The next thing he told me about James was that he needed time. I was not to call James at all but to wait for him to call me. This was a very difficult period. I wanted so badly to talk to him. Every day for a month, I waited for a call that never came. In my times of doubt, the Holy Spirit would always come and whisper to me that my future was in God's time, not mine. But there was so much I wanted to share with James. I wanted him to know my journey. I wanted to know what was happening in his world.

Finally, after a month, I got this very gentle nudging in my spirit that I could write all those things down and just keep the letters until after I talked to James again and then send them. So that was what I did.

Every day, sometimes twice a day, I would write letters to him, sharing with him about my life, my feelings, my plans, my hopes, and my dreams. For the very first time in my life, I was being open and honest with a man, and it felt wonderful. Diane was the only person with whom I had ever shared so deeply, but I trusted this man. I trusted God. I trusted our love for one another.

After a month of writing letters, I still had not heard from James. I was getting super anxious. I had learned that peace is the first fruit of the spirit and that if I felt peace, it was from God, and if I felt anxiety, I was off God's path. So, feeling anxious as I was driving to an appointment with Louise, I asked God if I was still supposed to be waiting for James to call. I prayed for him to guide me. I told Louise about my anxiety, and she suggested that maybe God was ready for me to call just to find out where James stood on things. I said I would consider that.

When I got home, I called Diane as I always do. When I mentioned that I was getting super anxious about things, she said that she had the feeling that it was time for me to call James. I have learned that God sometimes sends His messages through others, and this was two people in just over an hour telling me the same thing right after I had asked God for a sign. I didn't need a tree to fall on me to know what I was supposed to do.

The next morning, James and I talked for over an hour. It felt wonderful. He shared with me some things he wanted to do in life; we laughed, we joked, we were friends. He told me that it was fine to send the letters that I had written to him. I am sure he had no idea that he was about to get 150 pages, but as soon as I got off the phone, I mailed them all.

The second they were in the mailbox, I understood what all of the time between phone calls had been about. It was silent so I could write those letters. God shared with me that James, like many people, understands things better when he sees them in writing versus hearing them. It allows him to process the information. God wanted me to share everything in writing so that James could experience my thoughts, feelings, and ideas in the best possible way for him to receive the messages.

God also revealed that James needed a part of me that he could reach out to every day. James, being married, had no one except me to talk to about these things, and he couldn't fully express himself with me because it would violate his marriage commitment. These letters were a way to help him process who I am and what I mean in his life. This was confirmed in a later conversation he and I had when he told me he rereads those letters all the time. God's plans are so much bigger than we can understand.

Please go to www.yeahmetoobook.com to watch a short video with some behind-the-scenes information not included in the chapter.

What I Learned

God is always talking to us; we simply need to learn to listen. As I look back over not just this journey but all of my life, I realize that God is always talking to us through the Holy Spirit. The challenge for us is learning to hear Him and trust Him. He is here to guide us through life, but so often, we feel that we have to do life on our own, and He is only there to "oversee" things. I have learned that is so untrue. He is our partner, our guide, and our friend if we allow ourselves to be open to Him. What paths are opened to us when we allow God to be our tour guide through life?

To understand the right choices, search for peace. This was a HUGE learning for me. As I said, I learned that peace is the first fruit of the Holy Spirit. It is now my guidepost in life. At one point, I asked God to help me discern and understand His voice from my inner voice. His response was powerful and immediate. "Seek peace, and there you will find me." So many times, I have acted on my thoughts instead of feeling the power of peace and allowing it to guide my path. Where does peace guide you in your life?

God is ALWAYS on your side. As our heavenly Father, God is always not just focused on us but interested in helping us create the best possible outcome. He allows us to spread our wings and make mistakes, but He is also there to pick us back up, help us learn from those mistakes, and put us back on the path to happiness. With the understanding that God is on your side, what changes do you want to make in your life, and can you lean on your partner, God, to support you through the hard times?

Be patient and wait for God's timing. Okay, I will not even pretend that this is easy. It absolutely is not. Our human nature is to want things right now! We get to understand and trust that God has understanding about things that we can't begin to comprehend. My experience with James is a great example of that. He asked me to marry him at sixteen. At that point in my life, I was broken, lost, and desperate for anyone to pay attention to me and validate me. If I had married him at that point, I know without a doubt that I would have cheated on him and ruined everything. Not because I didn't love him but because I didn't love myself. Now that I have learned to love myself, I am ready to be the kind of wife he deserves to have. I also realize that as much as I want to be with him today, there are still things that he and I need to understand and experience before we are ready to be together. God's timing is always perfect, and I will wait for God's perfect timing rather than force my timing and settle for less than the best. Where in your life can you benefit from being patient and waiting for God's perfect timing?

CHAPTER 10
Faith Changes Everything

As all these things were going on with James, God was busy in other areas of my life as well. He wanted to transform my whole life, not just my love life. I need only follow His lead and have faith.

When God said He wanted me to spend time alone with Him, He meant it. Suddenly, everything in my business stopped flowing. I couldn't focus on my work as a sales coach. I had no prospects or leads. I began to have anxiety about money, and God showed me that I had almost $100,000 in credit available to me to live on while He and I were working together. He wanted me in Sanctuary with Him. I surrendered to Him and His will. From time to time, I would try to do things, and He would put roadblocks up to prevent it. It was much like I was an infant learning to crawl when you put soft borders around them so they can't get into anything that will hurt them. He kept me safe and protected in a world where He and I could work together, and I could learn how He was creating a new life for me.

The first thing I had to learn was what faith is about. It is what He is all about with us. He started sharing with me some messages about faith from the bible. I want to share some of them here with you and what I learned about those passages.

Jesus was walking through a crowd. A lady had been bleeding for twelve years and knew if she could just touch his robe, she would be healed. She reached out as he passed and touched his robe. He stopped. Even though

he was surrounded by people, he had known of her gentle touch because he said he felt the power leave him. His statement to her was, "By your faith, you are healed."

In Luke, it tells of Jesus healing a man with leprosy. Afterward, Jesus said to the man, "Rise and go. Your faith has made you well."

At another point, Jesus restored a man's eyesight. The words he spoke to the man were, "Receive your sight. Your faith has healed you."

Notice that each time, he didn't say, "I healed you," "God healed you," or anything like that. It was their faith that healed them.

In one of his many parables, he told of seeds being planted and what happened to them. He said that a seed planted in good soil would grow and flourish, and then he went on to explain that the seed planted in good soil with God was planted in those with faith.

Once again, he refers to the faith inside the person. God's work can only flourish in those who have faith.

When Jesus was asleep on the boat with the apostles, a storm came up. Even though they had seen him raise people from the dead, they woke him up terrified that they were going to die. He asked them, "Do you still have no faith?"

The power lies in faith. Jesus went to his hometown to minister to people there, but they didn't recognize him as the son of God. As a result, he left the town doing very few miracles. It says, "He was amazed at their lack of faith."

This was a powerful learning for me. It was the moment

when I realized that each of us prevents God from performing miracles for us every day when we lack faith. Even Jesus could not perform miracles because the people lacked faith. Our faith is what unleashes God's power and miracles in our lives.

At one point, Jesus says, "According to your faith, be it unto you."

In other words, you can have whatever you have faith in, provided you want it for the right reason.

In John 11:24, he even tells us what faith is. It says, "Whatever you pray for, believe you have received it, and it will be yours."

Faith is understanding that when you ask God for something, it is a done deal, maybe not in your time, but in His. These were the lessons being learned during my time in Sanctuary with God. I was beginning to understand that I held so much power in my life that I wasn't using. God wanted to unleash so many blessings on me, but my lack of faith was preventing it. The key to understanding faith and what life can hold for us is held in a single verse: "God's people have not because they ask not."

I had spent my life trying to carry the weight of the world on my shoulders. I thought that if I wanted something, I had to do it all. I worked hard, I dieted, I exercised, I did everything in my power, or so I thought, to create the life I dreamed of, full of love, laughter, health, and success. And that was the whole problem. I was trying to do it all. I didn't understand the one power I had that was lying dormant and unused. I hadn't unleashed my faith.

When I attended the transformational leadership course, they often discussed that we were all focusing on what we were doing instead of focusing on who we were being. I didn't get it. I couldn't understand what they meant. However, after understanding faith came the realization that I had spent my life as a human doing rather than a human being. To create the life of my dreams, my focus needed to be on who I was being rather than what I was doing. That single lesson began creating power in my life.

Slowly, I started looking around at my life and seeing that I had managed, with all of my hard work, to create the exact life that I didn't want. I was fifty six years old, overweight, on tons of medication to keep my health stable, financially unsuccessful, making just enough to get by, and alone. This is what lack of faith and being a human doing had created for me. Let me tell you, it sucks! But I'm sure some of you are looking around now and realizing the same thing, saying, "Yeah…me too."

I wanted a different life and now had the key to creating it: Faith. But how do you start to develop this faith? I'm no authority on the subject, but I can tell you that faith is like a muscle. The more you work it, the stronger it gets.

Reaching back in my memory, there was a book that a friend and mentor had recommended called *The Secret*. In this book, Rhonda Byrne talks about the power of the human mind to create. She gave the example of healing her poor eyesight. Using her technique, she had perfect vision in just three days. She called it the secret. I call it faith. She had unleashed God's miracle in her life through her faith that what she hoped for could be a reality. I decided if she could, then so could I. What follows are the areas of my life that have been transformed as my faith and trust in God grew.

Health and Wellness

As a young girl and young woman, I had perfect vision. Like most people, however, as I got older, it got worse. I had begun needing reading glasses years before this event, and it had progressed to the point where I couldn't even read the big print on a menu without them. It seemed like a great strengthening exercise for my faith, just as it had been for Rhonda.

The next morning, I simply said, "Thank you, God, for my perfect vision," as a part of my prayers. I stood in faith that He could and would restore my vision. That was on July 31st. I still needed my glasses for the next few days, but on August 3, I was able to open my bible and read even that tiny print without any reading glasses. Like the woman who had touched Jesus' robe, my faith had healed me. It was time to exercise my faith muscle and create the vision that God had shown me of the life he had in store for me.

I began praying over my health. Knowing the extra weight I was carrying wasn't helping my physical fitness, I started thanking him for allowing me to release the extra weight. Suddenly, I began to feel the need to move my body more. I exercise daily now. Previously, I had tried and hated exercise, so I wasn't consistent. Now everything is different. There have been days when I decided to take a day off from working out and just couldn't do it. I crave moving my body now and do it every day. I have begun slowly releasing those excess pounds.

I also began thanking God for returning my body to a state of perfect health without taking any medications. I knew and still know that He is healing my body daily. The proof of his miracles is evident.

Prior to this exercise of faith, I was taking two types of blood pressure medication. My blood pressure normally ran around 125/85, even with two medications. As soon as I started praying in faith, my blood pressure dropped dramatically to the point that I was getting dizzy. I bought a home blood pressure cuff, and instead of 125/85, my blood pressure cuff began giving me readings of 90/60. It was no longer high; it was low!! After stopping one of my medications for a month, it was still on the low side, reading an average of 100/65. Another month later, I dropped the second medication for a week, and my blood pressure readings were running around perfect at 110/70. Yet another health victory for God and my faith.

Having been on antidepressants for over 20 years, I became aware that it was time to lose that crutch as well. God had healed my body so that the serotonin was being properly produced and used. With the guidance of my therapist, I slowly decreased the amount of medication. I am overjoyed to report that I am now completely off my antidepressants and have honestly never felt happier and more well-adjusted in my life. God, for the win again!

My diabetes? Guess what? It is substantially improved. My A1C was at a 7.2. After I started praying, it dropped to 6.1. I watch my glucose levels daily now, staying steady at around 120, whereas before, it was steady at around 250. God is healing all of my body and my spirit. I have discovered that faith is the lever that moves the world.

Up until this point, I also had some pretty annoying digestive issues. Terrible gas all the time made me constantly belch. I took the generic version of Prilosec daily as well as taking a seemingly endless supply of antacid tablets (about 300 tablets a month), trying to keep as much under control as I could using medicines. It improved it a little, but it was still a daily challenge that was noticeable to everyone around me. After beginning to pray in faith, I no longer take any medication for it other than an antacid, maybe once a month. I no longer have any problems with gas.

For the last fifteen years, I battled a fairly serious case of irritable bowel syndrome that had me literally running to the bathroom multiple times per day. That, too, has completely stopped. My digestive system now functions completely normally.

It wasn't just my health that started healing after learning to pray in faith, however. God began transforming every part of my life.

You have already read about my sleeping issues. It had been a lifelong struggle to simply fall asleep. After being molested in bed at night as a little girl, my subconscious mind was hyper-vigilant at all times, but especially at night. Being on high alert, my brain wouldn't shut down. I was taking both melatonin and Benadryl nightly to fall and stay asleep. Even with the medicine, I wasn't resting because my brain was still on high alert, watching for danger.

I began praying to God to protect me while I slept. Prayer, in combination with a technique I learned where I scan my body, I now fall asleep quickly and easily each night. Sleep comes easily and allows me to wake up fully rested and ready for a new day. Rather than the 11-12 hours a night previously needed to get through each day, I now wake up without an alarm clock after about seven hours of sleep. It is like living a completely different life to feel awake and rested.

Social Interactions

The need to isolate myself has also shifted dramatically. I shared how I spent most of my time alone. I have always had very few close friends, but even with them, the connections were few and far between.

Why would I choose not to spend time with those few friends? Quite frankly, being around other people just exhausted me. I would talk to someone on the phone or go have lunch with them and come home needing a nap. Just being around others, even if I loved them, left me feeling completely depleted mentally, physically, and emotionally.

There was a single exception to this. My best friend Diane was different. Rather than leaving me exhausted, talking with her often energized me. I had no idea why; I just knew that she was the one I had always wanted to be around.

As this journey of healing unfolded, the realization hit me that something else about talking to Diane was different. Every time I talked to her, God started talking to me a mile a minute. Many times, she and I laughed about the fact that when we talked, suddenly God became Chatty Cathy.

One day, as we were talking, I laughed, saying, "Well, here comes Chatty Cathy again. I don't know why God always wants to talk to me when I talk to you." At that moment, God spoke very clearly to me. "Because with Diane, there are no walls." Instantly, the understanding hit me that God was always talking to me, but my walls were so high they even blocked God out. With Diane, I trusted her completely and didn't have my walls of protection up. As a result of being open and feeling safe, I could hear His voice.

This was followed up by another bomb from God. "And by the way, people don't exhaust you. Holding up the walls around people exhausts you." Complete Mic Drop!

Suddenly, it all made sense. When I was with anyone other than Diane, I felt vulnerable and unsafe. Anytime I was with anyone else, I spent my whole time holding up the walls I had built to keep me safe.

One of the coaches I worked with taught me that awareness is the win. This was a great example of that learning. Just understanding this one fact began to transform all of the relationships in my life. I prayed for God to give me the discernment and ability to create healthy boundaries in my life so that I didn't have to feel the need to hold up those walls all the time. I began to trust God to keep me safe instead of my false walls. It has allowed me to relax and let other people in.

It also allowed me to stop judging myself and others. Accepting myself and others as we are is a special gift all its own and creates a freedom that simply can't be described. It must be experienced.

I am happy to say that I now spend time with other people on a daily basis. I no longer spend days or even weeks without talking to anyone other than Diane. I talk to others on the phone, go out to lunch, attend get-togethers, go to the movies, sing karaoke, and attend many other social events. Even more interesting is the fact that I no longer feel exhausted afterward. I actually enjoy spending time with other people.

Being connected to others feels comfortable and joyful. Even large social events are no longer uncomfortable, awkward, and avoided if at all possible. I actually look forward to events and don't see them as simply a personal or business obligation. I enjoy attending social events and being around groups of people. I am happy to say that I am also 100% comfortable in those situations. Far from avoiding social situations, I now seek them out or initiate them.

Most importantly, I am no longer wearing a mask all the time. If I am smiling, it is because I am genuinely happy. If I am sad or upset, I share that openly and vulnerably. I can ask for support when I need it.

As you can see, God and my faith have totally transformed my social life. Instead of a self-conscious, fearful introvert, I have become a happy, confident social butterfly. I love being out of my cocoon.

Emotional and Physical Comfort

There is no longer a need to make self-deprecating jokes – especially before someone else has an opportunity to do so. I fully love and accept every part of who I am. When I look in the mirror, I see a beautiful, intelligent, sensitive, powerful woman, and I assume that's what everyone else sees as well. It has allowed me to take down the walls.

Controlling my anger has also been a huge life-changing event. I no longer explode in anger. Feeling safe and comfortable to share my viewpoints, I address things that bother me by talking about them when they happen, not waiting for them to build up until I just explode.

Incredibly, I now actually feel other emotions. I no longer think my way through life; I feel my way through. There are true connections with other people. I love the people in my life. I miss them when they aren't around, especially James. Learning to love him opened the door to love others and have strong relationships.

I used to be uncomfortable and cringe away from human touch and hugs as a way to show support and be supported. Touch was only part of sexual engagement. Thanks to the healing I experienced that is no longer the case. Giving and accepting physical contact is no longer a chore to be polite. It is a natural and beautiful part of my life.

Not only are my emotions available to me, but my physical sensations are returning. I am able to feel my physical body, both pain and pleasure.

As a result of being hit by the car, my doctor told me I would have arthritis in my hip by age eighteen. I had never experienced it at all. In the last six months, however, I now feel that pain in my hip and I am so excited by that. It sounds weird

124

to say you are grateful for the pain, but when you have spent a lifetime completely disconnected from your own body, pain is a very welcomed feeling. It also means feeling pleasure and fully experiencing who I am.

Love of Myself and Others

My faith and relationship with God also totally transformed the most important earthly relationship - my relationship with myself. I now give myself grace and space to grow. I don't beat myself up for every mistake but rather understand that mistakes are how we learn. I accept the mistake, take the lesson, and move forward.

I trust myself. It is part of why I am able to relax around others and not keep the walls up. I trust myself to make good decisions about who are good people to be around and to keep those who are not healthy for me at a distance. I trust myself to speak up when I am uncomfortable with something or disagree. I trust myself to gently push back when someone says something to me that has the potential to damage my self-esteem.

I also trust myself with my relationship with God. I no longer doubt that it is really Him when He talks to me. I trust that I have received the gift of discernment so that I can distinguish God's voice from my own and that my ability in that area grows every day. If I am ever unsure, I simply pray and allow God to show me the truth.

I allow myself to love others and to accept love from them. Rather than pushing away affirming words and compliments that come as statements of love and respect, I now accept them graciously and give them freely to others. Love flows abundantly in my life.

One of the most major shifts is being open to a romantic

relationship. I broke through the barriers of not trusting love and the idea that marriage was horrible. Now, I fully embrace the idea of James and I one day being in a loving marriage where there is trust, openness, and communication. I look forward to sharing my life with someone in a relationship where we can love and support one another.

While I am fully invested in the dream of James and me that God shared with me, I am also aware of other men who are attracted to me and want to spend time with me. This awareness is new to me. It is because I finally see myself as attractive, valuable, and lovable. Knowing that other men find me appealing is great for my ego and more evidence of my transformation.

I no longer feel the need to overcompensate for others to see me as valuable. There is no longer a drive to do more, love more, give more, and bring more to the table every day. Carrying the full weight of everything I am involved in is no longer my responsibility. I do my part and let others do theirs with no guilt or feeling like I need to do more to measure up. This, too, is incredibly freeing. Having a life outside of work means that I matter.

I have shed the need to be a Lone Wolf in everything I do. If I have more than I can handle, I am fully okay with asking those around me for support, whether that is work or personal. Asking for support is not a sign of weakness. On the contrary, it is a sign of both strength and inner security. I am very proud to say I now possess both.

Perception of Work and Money

How I look and think about work has also changed. I have finally broken through that $40,000-a-year barrier that held me back for so long. I have no problems at all sharing the cost of my coaching or speaking with others. I am confident that they will receive far more from our working together than the price of my time and, as a result, have no problem at all asking for the money. I am worth it.

My relationship with and thoughts about money have completely changed. Like many things in life, the shift happens so slowly that we sometimes don't recognize it until something calls it up to hit us in the face. That's what happened to me regarding money.

My whole life, my mother always used a paring knife to peel potatoes. I, on the other hand, used a vegetable peeler. It was annoying, took longer and made a mess, but it was the tool I always used. Then, one day, about six months into this transformation process, I realized that the past few times I had peeled potatoes, I had switched to using a paring knife.

It created curiosity in me to wonder why I would have switched subconsciously. Suddenly, God shared this amazing revelation with me. I had always used a vegetable peeler because it got only the peel, so there was no waste. A paring knife, while much easier to use, went deeper and "wasted" some of the potatoes. A subconscious shift regarding God's abundance had taken place, and as a result, I was now no longer living in scarcity all the time. I had come to accept God's abundance and altered my behavior accordingly.

Loving Myself in God's Image

Let me share a story with you to illustrate the greatest evidence of how I now love and accept myself fully. All of my life, I have used a compact mirror to put on my makeup. Often, people asked me how and why I did this. I told them that I had spent years traveling with a rock and roll band who wore more makeup than me. Mirror time was at a premium, so I learned to use a small mirror. All totally true facts, and it felt like the truth.

One day, about a year into this transformation, however, I realized that the last few times I had put on my makeup, I had been using the full mirror in my bathroom. It created another one of those curious moments. God revealed to me that in the past, I had used the tiny mirror, not because it was a learned behavior as I had always believed. The truth was that being so filled with self-hatred, looking at my full face, was too painful for me. I could only bear to see myself in tiny sections. His love and my faith had combined to transform that. I now love and accept myself fully. I can look at myself in the full mirror and find joy in who and what I am. Is there a greater gift than that?

As you can see, my life has completely changed.

- I now take risks that seemed impossible to face before.

- I don't feel the need to "be the best" and win at everything, but rather spend my time creating win/win situations.

- I fully love and accept myself.

- I feel safe and capable of making good decisions about everything.

- I understand my value both emotionally and financially.

- I take risks and make mistakes, understanding that mistakes are part of growth instead of an indictment of my value.

- I live a life of abundance.

- I lean into God for all things and follow the path that He has laid out for me.

- I am strong and healthy both mentally and physically without needing the support of medications.

- I focus on who I am being rather than what I am doing. I value myself and others.

- I don't need to "fix" anything in my world so that I feel like I am enough. I know I am enough.

I now allow myself to fully experience life and play a big game. In short, I am no longer hiding in the shadows. I now stand in the light and unapologetically be seen as I am. I recently heard a definition of freedom that I fully embody and embrace today. Freedom is being willing to allow others to misjudge you. I am so blessed to finally feel free.

With great faith, however, God creates tests, and I was no exception. With all of these amazing things happening all around me, it was time for me to have what I call an altar moment, and it was a doozy.

Please go to www.yeahmetoobook.com to watch a short video with some behind-the-scenes information not included in the chapter.

What I Learned

Faith is everything. Of all the things I have learned, this, in my opinion, is the most important. It is the absolute bottom line of this entire book. I tried many paths to heal from the traumas of my past. I had limited success with each of them, and they all played a part in getting me to where I am today. Nothing, however, has had the intensity and transformation that I have found in finding and exercising my faith in God and His power. There isn't even a close second. It has created transformation on a level I couldn't have even comprehended if I had not experienced it myself. If you take one thing from this book, my hope and prayer is that it is to seek God and learn to unleash the power of faith so you can watch miracles unfold in your life. Where do you want to see miracles in your life?

CHAPTER 11
A Moment at the Altar

Things were moving along in my friendship with James, and we talked from time to time. Diane and I decided to head north to see the fall foliage and Niagara Falls in mid-October. I told James that I would be in the area and would love to meet him for lunch if he were open to it. He said he'd think about it and wanted to know when I was coming. I didn't hear anything from him one way or the other, so the morning before I was heading in his direction, I called him. I told him I was going to be in the area the next day and asked if he wanted to see me. To my shock, he answered with a forceful "NO."

We talked, and the upshot of the conversation was that he didn't want to see me, didn't want me to call, and didn't want me to write. When I tried to understand what was going on, I was met with the statement, "I won't talk about this while I am married." That explained it all to me. James is a man of great honor and integrity and was unable to separate his love for me from friendship. To continue to have contact with me was a violation of his marriage vows and his commitment. It was a place he was unwilling to go.

This integrity was the very thing that I love most about him, and it is the very thing that is preventing us from even being friends. It was a bitter pill to swallow, but I also knew that it was what he needed. So, I am honoring his request and moving forward with the other plans God has me working on. So why did I call this an altar moment? In the Bible, God made Abraham a promise that he would have a son even though Abraham and his wife Sara were far past childbearing years.

Abraham stood in faith in this word, and Sara gave birth to a son ten years later and named him Isaac. Later, God asked Abraham to sacrifice Isaac to Him.

Can you imagine the faith that it took for Abraham to sacrifice not just lifelong dream of a child but his actual child? God delivered on his promise, and now he wanted to take that promise back. It was a true test of faith and love of God. What did Abraham want more? His promised son or God? Abraham chose God and was spared having to sacrifice Isaac.

That was the type of choice I was now facing with James. This love that I had found for James had pulled me into a world where God was and is the center of everything. This door had been opened by the promise God gave me that James was the man I was to marry and spend my life loving. And now, He was asking me to give that beautiful dream back.

The question was, what did I want more? Did I continue to hold onto James and attempt to figure out how to work toward the future that I was promised? Or did I let the dream go and follow whatever path God had for me?

As much as I love James, the choice was an easy one. No matter how much I wanted this man, I wanted God, His love, and His peace more. I have chosen to not fight but to surrender to God's will.

Does that mean that God lied to me when he showed me my wedding ring and told me that James and I would live in Holy Matrimony? Not at all. If that is His will, it will still happen. My role is not to do something to create that dream but to have faith that God will do it in his time. "Faith is the substance of things unseen, the evidence of things hoped for." God did not say it would happen immediately or in my time. He simply promised me it would be. I get to be patient and wait for God's divine timing. In the meantime, I get to pray for

His highest and best for James, his wife, and his family.

I don't begin to claim to understand God's plan and what my full part is in it. I simply know what was shared with me by the Holy Spirit. I stand in complete faith that before my journey on this earth is complete, God's promise to me will be fulfilled, and James and I will be husband and wife in God's kingdom. I am also willing to surrender that dream if it is His will.

In the meantime, I continue to follow God's breadcrumbs in my life. It is easy to believe what is obvious. That is not faith. Faith is holding to God's promise even when it doesn't look possible. I choose to live my life in unshakable faith.

As I am growing into understanding how God works, I realize that testing of faith is a constant in a relationship with God. The testing of our faith is not a bad thing. It allows us to be clear about where we are going and what we want in life. It reminds me of a story I heard years ago.

A lumberjack named John went to a logging camp and got a job. He wanted to be the very best lumberjack in the camp and set his sights on outperforming the top producer, Jake.

On the first day, John worked as hard as he could. When the end of the day came, they returned to camp. John had cut down six trees. When talking to Jake, he discovered that Jake had chopped down seven trees. Now John had a mark to aim for.

The next day, John worked even harder and didn't take any breaks. He didn't even stop for lunch. He worked the entire day without stopping. When the shift ended, he had again taken down six trees, and Jake had taken down seven. He was both frustrated and determined.

The following day, John got up an hour early, worked

through lunch and breaks, and stayed an hour later than everyone else. At day's end, he had managed to chop down only five trees while Jake had cut down eight. He was now more frustrated and more determined.

The next morning, John began working two hours early, took no breaks, and stayed three hours later than everyone else. When he returned to the camp exhausted, he only knocked down four trees, and Jake cut down eight again. He was overcome with exhaustion and emotion. He went to sit with Jake to find out his secret.

John explained how he had worked longer and harder every day and yet always chopped down fewer trees each day. Jake, on the other hand, continued to perform at a higher rate every day even though he worked much less. Jake looked at him and said, "At any point during these last days, have you stopped to sharpen your axe?"

I feel like that is what God is doing when we have these altar moments. He is helping us sharpen our axes. He is defining things in our lives concerning His big picture for us and the world.

We live in a busy, chaotic, ever-changing world. It is easy to lose direction and focus amidst all of these worldly events. If we focus on the wrong things, our choices are poor. When we can see clearly what is truly important to us, we make good decisions. He simply calls us to clarify that vision of what is important and where we are going to make sure we get what truly matters most to us. Those altar moments are what call each of us into our greatness.

Please go to www.yeahmetoobook.com to watch a short video with some behind-the-scenes information not included in the chapter.

What I Learned

The hardest moment to hold onto our faith is when we need to hold onto it most. The altar moments in our lives feel heartbreaking at the time. They are often the most difficult moments we ever face. Our earthly selves seek immediate fulfillment. When it is something we feel we have been promised and finally get it, it is almost unimaginable to then give it up. It feels as if God is being harsh and cruel. In truth, God is powerfully helping us to understand our values and what is most important to us. It is easy to give up something you don't want for something that you do want. What is hard is defining what you want more. Do you sacrifice your relationship with God and the promise His presence offers on the altar of immediate satisfaction? Those altar moments define not only our future but also who we are as both humans and spiritual beings. What will you decide when God asks you to give back your dream?

CHAPTER 12
The End? Not a Chance!

I hope that my journey and what I have learned so far has supported you in some way. My hope with this book is to let you know that you aren't a bad person, you aren't alone, you aren't crazy, and that it is possible to create the life you have always dreamed of having.

Have I arrived at my perfect life yet? Nope, not even close. I am still working on my health, my wealth, my relationships, and my faith. I don't think we ever finish that journey. It is an ongoing process that is ever-evolving. It's like taking a walk. The further you walk, the further you can see. Our vision, hopes, and dreams are always expanding. It is the challenge of reaching that next point that keeps us feeling alive and vital.

What I have reached, however, is self-confidence, self-love, love for those around me, absolute joy, and, most importantly, a powerful, loving, trusting relationship with God. Every day, I experience new things. I feel things I've never experienced. I can live in the world without those clothes that are four sizes too small and the mask that I always wore. I am me, and I love who I am!

There are a couple of learnings that came to me along the way that I haven't yet shared, but I feel it is vital that I tell you about them.

The most powerful skill we have is to listen. This applies to both people and God. Often in life, we are so busy trying to speak that we don't listen. There are lessons that we learn only from listening. And sometimes, it is not what they are saying, but what they aren't saying that matters most. Hear the truth that others are speaking to support your growth and also to support theirs. What you hear may change everything you think and believe. I learned this lesson from those three simple words: "Yeah….me too." They changed my entire life. What have we not heard from God or others because we were talking instead of listening?

You matter. Your presence matters. You get to stand up and take up space in this world. I believe that each of us has an important contribution that we were sent to make to the world. When we stay small, we cheat the world of this gift. Your growth and healing are not just important for you; they are important for all of us in the world. If you don't grow, the unique gift that you were sent to share with the world is never realized and cheats us all. God created you for a purpose. You get to stand up and fulfill it. What will you use your presence to create in this world?

I would be remiss if I didn't share with you a few short quotes that I have learned in my journey that have helped me to stand strong and find the next step. I hope you find value in them.

- What would I do right now if I were amazing? (Jim Stovall)

- Believe that great things can happen. (Billy Florence)

- Expect great things. (Ron Hale)

- God's people can have what they say, but they are too busy saying what they have. (Toby Hale)

- The enemy of great is not bad. The enemy of great is good. (Jim Collins)

- Fear is the enemy of success. (Tzu Sun)

- If you want something you've never had, you will have to do something you've never done. (Thomas Jefferson)

- Is the choice I am making right now moving me closer to or further away from what I want? (unknown)

- Freedom is being willing to allow others to misjudge you. (unknown)

And the one that I think taught me the most.

"Saying I will do something and completing it is NOT the same as saying I will do something and giving an excuse for why I didn't do it." This one caused me a great deal of trouble until I understood it. I had gone through most of my life acting as if they were the same thing. For example, saying I am going to make fifty calls and doing it is not the same as saying I would make fifty calls and not doing it because an emergency came up. Just the awareness changed a lot for me. I hope it helps you. I invite you to let that knowing sink in and allow it to change the way you approach life.

As I stated in the beginning, I hope that what I have shared will support you in your journey. I would love to hear what you learned or gained from this book. Please leave a review on Amazon to share what this book has taught you.

I also enjoy speaking to audiences about the topics I cover in this work. I find that connecting in person creates openings and opportunities that are transformative for both the speaker and the listeners. If you have a group that you feel could benefit from a live presentation, please feel free to contact me.

So, we have come to the end of my journey so far. It is

definitely to be continued, and I am super excited to find out what comes around the next curve. May our paths meeting create powerful change in the future for us both!

And for my fellow leadership graduates, I am a loving, powerful, passionate woman! YES, I AM!!

Please go to www.yeahmetoobook.com to watch a short video with some behind-the-scenes information not included in the chapter.

An Urgent Plea

Thank You for reading my book!

I love receiving your feedback and hearing what you
have to say.

I need your help to make this book and my future books
better.

Please take two minutes right now,
To leave some helpful feedback on Amazon.

Let me know what you thought about the book.

Thanks so much!!!

Sara P. Cozi

Made in the USA
Columbia, SC
25 September 2024

42354648R00080